IN THE FOOTSTEPS
OF
AN ANCIENT FAITH

IN THE FOOTSTEPS OF AN ANCIENT FAITH

Living the Ancient Wisdom in the Modern World

Charles R. Ringma

Regent College Publishing
www.regentpublishing.com

ALSO BY CHARLES R. RINGMA

Catch the Wind: A Precursor to the Emergent Church

Cry Freedom: With Voices From the Third World

Dare to Journey with Henri Nouwen

Finding Naasicaa: Letters of Hope in an Age of Anxiety

Hear the Ancient Wisdom: A Meditational Reader for the Whole Year from the Early Church Fathers up to the Pre-Reformation

Hear the Heart Beat with Henri Nouwen

Let My People Go with Martin Luther King Jr.

Life in Full Stride: Faith-Stretching Reflections for Christians in the Real World

Ragged Edges: Poems from the Margins

Resist the Powers with Jacques Ellul

Seek the Silences with Thomas Merton

Seize the Day with Dietrich Bonhoeffer

Wash the Feet of the World with Mother Teresa

Whispers from the Edge of Eternity: Reflections on Life and Faith in a Precarious World

For
Russell and Kay Brothers
and
Peter and Glenda Bryant
and
Caleb Kak-Sin Koo and Grace Shangkuan Koo,
*who, among others, have made possible
my many teaching and ministry trips into Asia
for the past twenty-five years.*

Copyright © 2015 Charles R. Ringma

All rights reserved. No part of this publication may be reproduced, stored in a retrieval system, or transmitted, in any form or by any means, electronic, mechanical, photocopying, recording or otherwise, without the prior written permission of the author, except in the case of brief quotations embodied in critical articles and reviews.

Published 2015 by Regent College Publishing

Regent College Publishing
5800 University Boulevard, Vancouver, BC V6T 2E4 Canada
Web: www.regentpublishing.com
E-mail: info@regentpublishing.com

Regent College Publishing is an imprint of the Regent Bookstore <www.regentbookstore.com>. Views expressed in works published by Regent College Publishing are those of the author and do not necessarily represent the official position of Regent College <www.regent-college.edu>.

ISBN 978-1-573-83456-8

Cataloguing in Publication information is on file at Library and Archives Canada.

CONTENTS

Preface 9

Introduction 13

1 Longing: Leaning into God's Future 21

2 Finding: The Quest for Homecoming 39

3 Journeying: Spiritual Pilgrimage 56

4 Wondering: The Gift of a Child-like Faith 74

5 Celebrating: A Life of Gratitude 92

6 Praying: Nourishing the Inner Life 109

7 Purifying: Embracing the Gift of Purgation 127

8 Contemplating: Seeing All Things with New Eyes 145

9 Joining: The Mystery of Community 164

10 Serving: The Joy of Self-Giving 182

11 Mourning: Grieving Loss 199

12 Waiting: Living in Expectation 218

Afterword 237

Endnotes 239

Preface

This book is the final companion to *Life in Full Stride* and *Whispers from the Edge of Eternity.* For some reason, I like trilogies.

While the above-mentioned books draw their inspiration from the biblical narrative and a wide range of Christian sources, *In the Footsteps of an Ancient Faith* draws exclusively from scripture and pre-Reformation Christianity, beginning with the writings of the early church fathers through to the late medieval Christian mystics.

I certainly regard the Reformation and its subsequent developments as important, and these writings have shaped my Christian formation. But as a Protestant Christian, one should not stop at the Reformation. For the "communion of saints," which we all confess in the Apostles' Creed, calls us into solidarity with the whole of the Christian tradition—not only a part of it. The Reformers themselves were deeply indebted to the early church fathers. Thus the martyrs, monks and mystics are part of our Christian heritage—God's gift to us—and we do well to glean from their fourteen hundred years of wisdom.

When we read from the early church fathers, the Desert hermits, the monastic tradition and the Christian medieval mystics, we drink from ancient wells of faith and prayer and are refreshed by cool subterranean water. These ancient voices come to us in our modern world like whispers from another world, resonating with our longing for older sources of inspiration and spirituality.

This, of course, is not to suggest that these ancient voices are "pure" fountains of inspiration. For all was not well and wonderful with that ancient world, as we know from its patriarchal traditions and general exclusion of women, the church's grab for political power and the madness of the Crusades. But in the midst of an often barren religious landscape, some ancients sang songs of hope and renewal that can continue to encourage us in our times.

In turning to this ancient wisdom, I am not proposing a "quick-fix" for our present-day spiritual challenges. For to make our way in the contemporary world, we will need to be sustained and challenged by the old, but empowered by the life-giving Spirit to apply that wisdom to our contemporary context.

Nor am I suggesting that modern Christianity is bankrupt. For Christianity in the non-Western (Majority) world has an inspirational vitality. And the somewhat battered and tired Christianity in the Western (Minority) world is searching and praying for renewal, revitalization and the gift of reenchantment. Yet modern Christianity has been far too

PREFACE

beholden to attacks upon it from the Enlightenment, and as a consequence, the church has become far too defensive, inward-looking and rationalistic. Christians have become comfortable dancing to the Enlightenment's tune.

But new winds are blowing all over the world and in communities of faith. Through the ever-renewing breath of the Holy Spirit, there are strains of a new melody line: not mere rationalism, but wisdom; not mere activism, but contemplation; not mere explanation, but mystery; not mere institutionalism, but community; not skepticism, but hope; not complacency, but depth; not manipulation, but vulnerability; and not programmatic religious strategies, but the heart-cry for a new spirit.

This new melody, while holding to the importance of the historic creedal statements of the church, sings of longing, journeying, accompanying, exploring, crying, hoping for God to bring us all into the Spirit's restorative and mending work for all humanity and all creation. This melody belongs to all of us, irrespective of our religious traditions. We all long for a better world. We all live in hope. We all cry out to be healed from the pains of our fractured world and our often dysfunctional relationships.

In turning to this ancient wisdom, I hope fellow travelers will find inspiration and spiritual sustenance. I also hope it will act as a mirror, allowing us to see our present-day faith

PREFACE

more clearly. And I hope that it will act as a large invitational letter, inviting us into a faith marked by martyr blood, intentional community and insights into the ways of God through contemplation and ecstasy.

May this meditational reader guide you into the deeper eddies of the mystery and revelation of God's love in Christ through the ever-renewing work of the Holy Spirit.

The words of the prophet Jeremiah may be appropriate as you engage this ancient faith:

> "Stand at the crossroads, and look,
> and ask for the ancient paths,
> where the good way lies; and walk in it,
> and find rest for your souls." (Jeremiah 6:16)

Some thanks are in order. First of all, Karen Hollenbeck-Wuest has cast her careful editorial eye over this work. Thank you, Karen! Secondly, a big thank-you to Bill Reimer and the team at Regent College Publishing to take this book on board. And finally, my heartfelt thanks to the "holy" scribblers: Irene Alexander, Chris Brown, Neville Carr, Terry Gatfield, Jill Manton and John Steward, who are my writing companions, and who first responded with challenge and insight to sections of this meditational reader.

Introduction

These reflections on the ancient wisdom, from the early church fathers to the medieval Christian mystics, cover nearly fourteen hundred years of writings from the pre-modern world. As such, these writings reflect a very different social world and a different way of thinking about and living the Christian faith.

In these pages you will meet some figures from the past who are probably well known to you: St. Augustine (354–430), St. Bernard of Clairvaux (1090-1153), Hildegard of Bingen (1098–1179), St. Francis of Assisi (1181–1226), and Julian of Norwich (c.1342–c.1413). But you may also meet those who are unfamiliar: St. Columbanus (c.540–615), St. Cyril of Alexandria (died 444), St. Isaac the Syrian (died c.700), Richard Rolle (c.1295–1349) and Geert de Groote (1340–1384). These and many others have not only survived in the witness of history, but their influence also continues to inspire and challenge us, calling us to live the faith with greater fidelity.

All of these writers were deeply steeped in the biblical story. Many quote scriptures from memory, and their writings weave scripture passages with their own reflections, pastoral concerns, and engagement with the issues of their time. Scripture for them was a normative narrative, which they sought to live with faith and courage. Scripture was not simply a guide, but the very voice of God.

This poses a challenge for our contemporary culture, because we hardly read scripture at all. Rather than inhabiting the narrative of the Bible, we tend to stand above it with our modern interpretive questions and concerns about historicity and literary styles. As such, we tend not to hear scripture as the word of God, but treat it as a spiritual resource that we can access when we need it or feel like it. Without a clear voice that calls and challenges us, we may be more lost than we realize.

What is particularly moving in these ancient writings is the way in which these authors sought intimacy with God. The word led to the God of the word, and these ancients sought to know and love this God as the deepest reality of their lives. God was at the centre, not the periphery, of who they were and who they sought to be. With some, this intimacy was expressed in martyr blood; with others, it was fulfilled in a monastic community; others deepened their union with God through mystical experiences. Their quest was to be so close to God that they would lose themselves in God. God was their greatest longing, their all in all.

INTRODUCTION

In our contemporary world, we are often more concerned with how God is blessing us than with being close to God. We may be concerned about the church and our mission in the world, but we are not too concerned about our union with God. We don't love God for who God is, but for the blessings he gives. We are not in the service of God, but we want God to support us. Thus we have pushed God to the periphery.

For our ancient forebears, this quest for union with God was a costly affair, requiring a life of holiness, sacrifice and relinquishment. Those who sought to know God more fully were willing to go into the desert to pray. They were willing to live in monastic communities. They were willing to fast. They observed a variety of spiritual practices. Theirs was a committed discipleship, where being ascetic provided space for the fuller presence of God. God had given new life to them, and they were willing to give their all for God.

We can only aspire to this in contemporary Christianity, for we care more about much-having than living a spirituality of relinquishment. Asceticism is not *our* favourite word, and discipleship is a concept that has fallen out of our daily vocabulary. Since Christian formation is no longer a standard practice in our community of faith, we make our own way in the spiritual journey. And so we have become spiritual orphans, rather than spiritual pilgrims.

INTRODUCTION

Here our forebears can point the way for us. We, too, need to be grounded in the word of God. We need to be formed in Christian community. We need companions on the journey. We need to grow in conformity to Christ. We need to be embedded in spiritual practices if our lives are to be fruitful in the service of Christ. This will call us away from our individualism and self-determination into relationship, mutuality and care for one another.

But neither hunger for scripture, nor the quest for union with God, nor a life of committed discipleship, nor engaging with certain spiritual practices caused our spiritual forebears to claim special status with God. They had no sense of a final arrival, nor did they claim mastery over God. Rather, they celebrated the mystery of God. Some highlighted that the movement in the spiritual life is not primarily a movement from darkness to light, but from light to darkness. For the closer one moves towards God, the greater God's incomprehensibility becomes.

This, too, challenges us, for we are quick to market our ways with God. We develop schemes about how God works, and we promote strategies about how to pray or how we should witness. But God will ever elude us, and our need for control will have to give way to a newfound humility.

While there were some unhealthy dualistic emphases in earlier Christianity, we can learn much from our ancient

INTRODUCTION

forebears' sacramental view of life. They honored all of life as sacred, having been marked by God's creative and sustaining activity. Even the ordinary was charged with God's grandeur, and they recognized their call to live the ordinary in prayer—and to a live a life of prayer in the ordinary. They knew well the reality of work as well as the call to prayer.

We can also learn from our ancient forebears' integrated spirituality, for they recognized that love of God also meant love of neighbour. Their lives in community involved the practice of hospitality. The practice of prayer included prayer for the world. Contemplation was not only the vision of God, but the contemplation of all things, including the neighbour in need.

Yet ours is a largely secular view of life and an inward spirituality. Thus we are happily schizophrenic. God is in our prayer chamber and the church but absent from life in general. Clearly, we need to recover a sacramental view of all of life, including the sacraments and the community of faith. We need to see all that is with this ancient vision as we attend to the signs of God's goodness, grace and love in our modern world. We cannot divide our lives into the secular and sacred, for all is sacred in the love of God.

We can also learn from the ancients' desire to enter into the whole life of Christ, including his suffering. This will challenge us not only to be part of the church, but also to

INTRODUCTION

bear its weaknesses. It will challenge us to embrace the dark night of the soul as well places of forsakenness. This call will beckon us to join with the suffering God for our world as we discover joy in serving the poor and needy.

As we join our ancient forebears in these reflections, may their voices find a way into our hearts. May we be renewed through their inspiration. May their goodness spill over into our lives. May our revitalization bring hope and goodness to our weary world.

* * *

These reflections invite slow, meditative reading, thus I hope you will be able to take them into the quiet spaces of your busy life. These reflections also might serve you in the setting of a personal or group retreat or for small group discussions.

Through reading this book meditatively, I hope the reflections may act as a springboard, where you "hear" more than what is written in these pages as the Spirit leads and guides you. This interactive way of reading is meant to lead you further in your journey of faith.

While it is possible to present the ancient wisdom under the headings of the inner and outer life or in terms of various spiritual practices, I have chosen to use the more dynamic

INTRODUCTION

concepts of longing, journeying, celebrating, purifying, among others. These concepts connect with all readers, for we are all on a search for meaning, and we all long for transcendence—including those in other faith traditions.

Finally, I am not trying to present systematically the theology and spirituality of the early church fathers, the Desert Fathers and Mothers, the monastics and the medieval Christian mystics. What I offer here is a mere sampling, but one that I hope will beckon you further into the depths of this ancient wisdom.

1

LONGING:

Leaning into God's Future

Longing is intrinsic to the human condition. While Descartes promulgated the idea, "I think, therefore I am," with its resultant emphasis on rationalism, we may instead say, "I long, therefore I become." This recognizes the future-oriented nature of the human being and also opens up the dynamic of human development. While Descartes' concept is more static, the latter is dynamic and unfolding.

There are no limits to human longing. We long for more or something else, even when we already have much. But human longing comes most clearly to the fore in settings of deprivation.

Imagine being lost without water and food supplies in the vast and unforgiving wasteland of the red centre of Australia with its soaring temperatures. One is usually dead within forty-eight hours. One longs for water. One longs to be found. One longs for one's mother. One longs for a miracle. The list goes on.

IN THE FOOTSTEPS

Obviously, this is an extreme setting, so why do we still long when our basic needs are not only met, but we have much? Though we may have prominence in our respective area of human endeavour, we are still filled with longings. Though we may be rich in relationships, we still long for more or deeper friendships. Though we may have an abiding spirituality, we continue to long for greater meaning in our lives and the world. Within a Christian framework, why do we long for God when God has already brought us "home"? How can one long for what one already has?

There are number of ways to consider these questions. The most basic is that whatever we have, we don't have in fullness. Riches can be lost, and there is always more to gain. Relationships are fragile, even when they are enduring. Our relationship with God is only ever partial, given the wholly Other nature of who God is. Thus having tasted, we long for more.

Said another way, since we have lost our archetypical "home" in the Garden of Eden, we are forever longing to find it again or to find what most closely approximates this utopian beginning. This longing is thus primordial. We are forever looking, forever longing, and we are never fully satisfied with whatever we find, for that "home" is lost to us forever.

This perspective has us looking backward, but another perspective points us forward. As human beings, we are future-oriented, eschatological creatures. We strain forward into a further becoming. We stretch ourselves towards self-fulfillment.

LONGING: LEANING INTO GOD'S FUTURE

We want an expanded and enhanced self. We long for a final consummation. Thus, even though we are already found in Christ by faith in the Spirit, we long for a fuller participation in the life to come.

Whatever explanations we may come up with, one thing is clear. Even the saints of old, who spoke of remarkable experiences with God, continued to hunger and search for God. We can hardly be different.

1.1 *The Longing Heart*

Good Protestant theology emphasizes the three-fold dance of the follower of Christ: justification, sanctification and glorification. This movement recognizes a life-long and eternal process of becoming more God-like, which is based on the theological premise that God became human so that we might become more Godly.

Yet contemporary Christianity has lost the idea of the process or shape of the Christian journey. In this dance routine, you are either in or out. If you're in, your worries are over and you settle in for a long ecclesiastical ride.

The contemporary church often fails to help us negotiate the contours of our faith journeys. Pastors seldom speak of the phases and transitions of the Christian life. Our faith communities don't form us more deeply into the life of Christ, nor train us in the practice of spiritual disciplines. Rather than fanning the flame of our longing hearts, the church often teaches that when we come to true faith in Christ, all our longings cease.

Yet our longing *begins* when we find the Christ, the Lamb of God, who takes away the sin of the world (John 1:29). And this is also true for those who are on other spiritual journeys. The beginning of enlightenment is not the end of the process.

LONGING: LEANING INTO GOD'S FUTURE

The early church fathers, monastics and medieval Christian mystics understood this longing well and expressed it as a quest for union with God. While some seemed to blur the distinction between the Creator and the creature, most spoke about this quest in more paradoxical terms.

St. Catherine of Genoa (1447–1510), a mystic and minister to the sick and dying, writes: "My Being is God, not some simple participation but by a true transformation of my Being." Then she goes on to say, "I clearly recognize now that all good is in God alone, and that in me, without divine grace, there is nothing but deficiency."[1]

Central to this quest for union with God is the longing heart. St. Augustine, the famous Bishop of Hippo in North Africa, writes, "Give me a man [woman] in love; he [she] knows what I mean. Give me one who yearns; give me one who is hungry; give me one far away in this desert who is thirsty and sighs for the spring of the Eternal country."[2] The more we feel this "desert" experience of being "far away" and disconnected from contemporary values, the more we long for a final homecoming.

The longing St. Augustine describes is not simply about coming to faith in Christ. Rather, it is a longing for a deeper communion, a quest for intimacy, a desire to lose oneself in the great "I am that I am" (Exodus 3:14).

Moses longed to see the face of God (Exodus 33:17–23); the Psalmist longs for God's presence (Psalm 42:1–2); Isaiah is overwhelmed by the holiness of Yahweh (Isaiah 6:1–5); Paul prays that we may be filled with all the fullness of God (Ephesians 3:14–19). These longings come out of our poverty—even though we are rich in Christ. They stem from our wanderings—even though we are already found. They well up out of our hunger—even though we have partaken of the Bread of Life. They are shaped by our desire to reconnect with a spiritual version of our mother's womb, which formed and held us.

When our longings are moved by love, they move towards consummation. We not only desire to be *with* Christ, but to be *in* Christ (John 17:21) and *in* the Spirit (1 Corinthians 12:13). Such an indwelling is not simply a belief *about* Christ, but a profound Christo-mysticism.

The longing heart is hungry for communion and homecoming—and the greatest homecoming is to overcome our archetypal alienation from the presence of God in the garden of Eden.

Reflection

St. Anselm (c.1033–1109), theologian and
archbishop of Canterbury, put it well:
"Always filled, always you drink."[3]

LONGING: LEANING INTO GOD'S FUTURE

1.2 *Impartation*

In the quest for union with God, our ancient forefathers and foremothers resorted to certain formulas meant to help the seeker in his or her growth in Christlikeness. They spoke of the value of celibacy, contemplative practices and of ascending ladders to indicate one's growth in spirituality.[4]

But most of our spiritual forebears had no illusions about negotiating various stages and so making it closer to God. St. Catherine of Genoa confesses, "From time to time I feel that I am growing only to see that I still have a long way to go."[5] St. Catherine's fellow Christian, the mystic Marguerite Porete (who was burned at the stake some time after 1312), wrote, "Lord, how much do I comprehend of your power, of your wisdom, and of your goodness? As much as I comprehend of my weakness, of my foolishness, and of my wickedness."[6]

Thus the quest for union with God is not simply a strategy with fine-tuned formulas. Growth in relationship with God is a graced journey deeper into the mystery of love, which may lead us to deserts and dark places. This quest is the fruit of what God imparts. It is the unfolding of God's life and ways in us. And this impartation of new life may well occur in the most unlikely or most difficult places in our lives.

While there has undoubtedly been the mysterious prior workings of the Spirit in our lives, which John Wesley called prevenient grace,[7] the foundation for the unfolding of God's life in us is the death of Christ on our behalf (Romans 3:21–26) and our being brought home to God to become "a dwelling place for God" (Ephesians 2:19–22). God has made us alive in Christ (Colossians 2:13) and we have come to fullness of life in Christ (Colossians 2:10). We are to continue to live in Christ and to be "rooted and built up in him" (Colossians 2:7). This involves the movement of putting off what is earthly and ungodly in us (Colossians 3:5–11) and garbing ourselves in the virtues of Christ-likeness (Colossians 3:12–17).

Thus we are to grow up into what we have been given and what has been imparted to us by the Spirit. Though Christ takes form in us (Galatians 4:19) and the Spirit is generous with us (Galatians 5:22–25), we will not grow if we do not worship, pray, fellowship, commune and love those in the community of faith as well as the stranger through our actions (Galatians 6:10).

This journey of faith is a life of joy, worship, discipline and costly service that is sustained by God's grace. We do not climb up to God; rather we embrace the wildly extravagant, descending God (Philippians 2:1–11), who surprises us and lifts us up. The unknown author of *The Cloud of Unknowing* (a fourteenth-century English mystical treatise) captures this well: "One loving blind desire for God alone is more valuable in itself, more pleasing to God and the saints, more beneficial to your own growth…than anything else you could do."[8]

This extravagant statement alone should remind us that a growing intimacy with God is beyond our careful strategies. While we should adopt a life shaped by the spiritual disciplines, the Spirit draws us into the life and mystery of the Trinity, our true home. Who knows what the breath of the Spirit may awaken and where it may blow us?

Reflection

Meister Eckhart (c.1260–1327), the
German Dominican mystic, says it well:
"To seek nothing and to set out only for God himself
is to discover God who gives the seeker all
that is in his divine heart."[9]

1.3 *Enamoured with God*

The way of life in late modernity is characterised by suspicion, fragmentation, self-interest and utilitarianism. We relate to others not with a caring friendship, but in the hope that they will benefit us in certain ways. It is not surprising, therefore, that we treat God in similar ways. God is hardly the Lord of our lives. God is simply our great beneficiary.

This is the longing heart turning in on itself. And it is a far cry from the quest for union with God. Our orientation is not towards God but towards ourselves, and we only relate to God to mine him in the similar careless ways in which we plunder the earth of its irreplaceable resources.

This, of course, is not to suggest that God's good gifts are unimportant, for they sustain our very lives and are a window into the heart and mystery of God. Thomas à Kempis (c.1380–1471), a member of the Brethren of the Common Life known for his *The Imitation of Christ,* encourages Christ followers well when he writes: "Set aside an opportune time for deep personal reflection and think often about God's many benefits to you."[10] These benefits are many: the gift of life, the produce of the earth, the blessings of family, the gift of friendships. Everywhere, there are the signs of God's generosity and care.

LONGING: LEANING INTO GOD'S FUTURE

In this frame, we can speak about the economic Trinity and Kataphatic spirituality. Simply put, God can be known through what God says and does. Who God *is* and what God *does* are entirely consistent. The one reflects the other. Thus we can know God through all his works (Job 37:14).

But God's works do not fully reveal who God *is*, for God is greater than all he has created (1 Kings 8:27), and we need to be careful that we don't see God merely for what God *does*. We should long for the mystery of his being. In this regard, Thomas à Kempis points us in another direction, noting that: "A wise lover considers not so much the lover's gift as the giver's love. He [she] attends more to the giver's affection than to the gift's value."[11] Indeed! See the one who loves you and not only what your lover may give you.

This calls us to a new way of being with God. For this is about friendship, not benefits and blessings. This is about the love of the Lover, not about the goodness that comes from such a relationship. This is all about the Other, not simply about me.

One small way to move into this kind of relationship is to recognize that God is well beyond our thoughts and the image of God we have in our minds. As St. Anselm confesses, "I only saw you in a certain degree, not as you are."[12] The English Christian mystic, Richard Rolle, emphasizes, "God is truly of infinite greatness, better than we think; of unreckoned sweetness; inconceivable of all natures wrought; and can never be comprehended by us as he is in himself in eternity."[13]

The God who is beyond all his gifts and beyond our knowing is not a God we can grasp, control or manipulate. Before this God, we must let go of our images of God and enter the wide spaces of the seeking heart. For such a God we can only wait in grateful expectation. This journey will lead us to surrender so that we may bow before the mystery of God, to worship and adore him. This God can only reveal himself in love—not in the fullness of his being—for we would surely die in the glory of such an unveiling.

To live with devotion to who God is, not simply concerned about his gifts, will draw us to care about what God wants rather than focusing on our own needs.

Reflection

The unknown author of
The Cloud of Unknowing reminds us:
"Go beyond your intellects endless and involved
investigations and worship the Lord your
God with your whole being."[14]

1.4 *Birthing*

The God of the Bible does not live in remote isolation, but rather engages us and the creation. God brings forth and renews through the work of creation and redemption.

In relation to Christ's salvific and healing work, St. Anselm writes, "And you Jesus, are you not also a mother? …For, longing to bear sons [daughters] into life, you tasted death, and by dying you begot them."[15] Clearly, Jesus has agonized us into life. The Spirit's gift is birthing.

The theme that through suffering we have been born to new life is everywhere in the pages of the New Testament. We are baptized into Christ's death and raised with Christ in newness of life (Romans 6:3–4). We are born anew through "water and the Spirit" (John 3:5). We are "born of God" (1 John 3:9) and born again "through the word of God which lives and abides forever" (1 Peter 1:23–25).

If God's nature is to bring forth, then we are also called to be generative. Not only are we invited to bring forth the next generation (Genesis 1:28), we are also called to be spiritually fruitful (John 15:5).

The Apostle Paul speaks of being like one in the pains of childbirth so that Christ may be formed in those for whom he had pastoral responsibility. His language is poignant as he describes feeling "the pain of childbirth until Christ is formed in you" (Galatians 4:19–20). This birthing is ongoing, for formation is an ongoing process.

Through friendship, pastoral care and mentoring, we can offer practical support and spiritual nurture for others. But we may also be called to be spiritual "seers" of our time, devoting our lives to the "hidden" service of discernment. Hildegard of Bingen, Abbess of Rupertsberg and advisor to kings and popes, speaks of patriarchs and prophets, "eminent men [women], who traversed the hidden ways and looked with the eyes of the spirit." They looked "in lucent shadows [and] announced the Living Light."[16] Clearly the church and world need seers: women and men who gaze into a world that may yet be. This is the gift of prophecy.

One may also be called to a "hidden" life of prayer in order to pray the "new" into being. St. Augustine says, "As for myself I will enter my closet and there sing to thee the songs of love, groaning with groanings that are unutterable now in my pilgrimage."[17] This form of prayer is also the language of birthing.

Whether one is deeply immersed in contemplation or in the costly work of justice, the call is to bring healing and renewal to our tired world. Whatever one's call may be, there is the challenge to remain faithful and committed. One of the Desert Fathers puts this clearly: "What therefore thou findest that thy soul [is] desiring in following God, that do, and keep thy heart."[18] One does not quickly bring forth the "new." For a long period of gestation is necessary to bring God's good into our world. This is the path of prayer and a long obedience.

Reflection

St. John Chrysostom (c.347–407), Bishop of
Constantinople and a fiery preacher, reminds us:
"One table is set for all, one Father begot us,
we are all born of the same birth pangs."[19]
And we, too, are called to bring a world
of equity and equality into being.

1.5 *Seeking the Kingdom of God*

The great longing of the Christian is not only to be released from the worries of this life in order to enter the bliss of the life to come. For the Christian also longs for the Kingdom of God to come more fully in the here and the now.

The Kingdom of God is not a spacial realm, but the very presence of God. And this presence appears wherever and whenever God is active in the world through the Holy Spirit, whether in the midst of the community of faith or apart from it. Since the Kingdom of God is always a greater reality than the church, the people of God are called to fidelity to the King of this kingdom.

Seeking the Reign of God is, first of all, the call to prayer and contemplation, and this is the movement of transcendence. In this move, we long to be with God face to face. But as Geert de Groote has rightly pointed out, the movement of transcendence must be completed in the move to incarnation. He writes: "Let me first seek the Kingdom [of God] and then I shall so much the better be able to serve my neighbor."[20]

This fourteenth-century founder of the Brethren of the Common Life points out that our inspiration and energy must first and foremost come from God. We move from contemplation to action. Meister Eckhart makes a similar point: "If they get no taste for divine sweetness, they drag;

LONGING: LEANING INTO GOD'S FUTURE

but if they lie in wait until they catch a taste of the divine, ever afterwards they become glad seekers of God."[21] And by way of extension, thus inspired, the followers of Christ will seek to be a blessing to others. Service is thus an overflow from prayer.

To long for the Kingdom of God is to live beyond self-preoccupation. Yes, the kingdom is within us and impacts us personally (John 3:5). But the kingdom is also amongst us (Luke 17:21) through the healing and renewing acts of Christ through the Spirit (Luke 10:9). Most basically, the Kingdom is God's lordship being manifested in our refractory and broken world.

To be shaped by the Kingdom of God and to bear its potentialities and burdens means that, as people of prayer and action, we will seek a better world, one of righteousness, peace and justice. To live this calling well, we need both insight and inspiration. St. Bernard of Clairvaux, who made Cistercian Monasticism a major force in Europe, points us in the right direction: "The revelation which is made by the Holy Spirit gives light so that we might understand, and fire so that we might love."[22] It is one thing to have passion. One also needs wisdom.

While there are many references in the parables of Jesus to the mysterious workings of Reign of God, we are called to enter the Kingdom and to become the servants of the

Kingdom (Luke 10:9). Because the Kingdom can never be our project and something we can control, we need light and passion, as St. Bernard has pointed out. Light is necessary so that the direction of our service is in conformity with the mission and ministry of Jesus. And passion is called for so that we might be empowered to walk the long road of the work for justice. To follow Christ with our lives, our minds, hearts and hands will need to be formed by him. Knowledge, passion and practicality combine in our call to witness and service.

Thus as servants of the Reign of God, we long for insight and discernment in order to know what to do—and we long to be sustained in our journeys of faith, witness and service. Thus prayer marks our calling and direction, and it sustains us in the long unfolding of this call to pour out our lives in the service of Christ.

Reflection

St. Bernard of Clairvaux:
"The one who understands truth without living it,
or loves without understanding,
possesses neither the one nor the other."[23]

2

FINDING:

The Quest for Homecoming

We cannot turn to the topic of finding apart from the subject of longing, for these two themes do not cancel each other out. Even when we "find" what we are longing for, it is not the "end" of the story, for our longings do not cease. Thus our finding is never complete, and our homecoming is never final. We find something of ourselves in a crisis, but there is always more to be found. We may find God in a revelatory experience, but we have only begun to know the edges of God's ways. We may find a precious metal after years of exploration, but there may be more to find. We may make a scientific discovery, but this may be only a small step in a long chain of discoveries yet to be made.

Finding something is exciting and important, for it is a stepping stone towards further insight, for which we can be ever grateful. But there often comes a temptation, which must be resisted, to let that discovery become a terminus for further exploration. In this sense, finding can be counter-productive, even unhelpful and dangerous.

In the Christian story, the theme of the biblical narrative is not first of all about finding, but of being found. God is the Hound of Heaven. Christ is the Good Shepherd, seeking that which was lost. And the brooding Spirit is ever at work in seeking us out.

Second, many theologians speak of the idea that in finding God, we also find ourselves. And the writers of Christian spirituality describe the search for our true selves as the pathway to God. By way of extension, we may say that if we truly know and love ourselves, we can also love our neighbours.

Third, finding God is an eschatological foretaste of the future life. Finding is thus a promise of what is yet to come. Finding opens a further future.

As we explore some of these themes in the following reflections, it is important to remember that finding is never simply a rational activity. Sometimes we don't know what we are looking for, but we search none-the-less. And the search is seldom a nice straight line. Often the discovery is the surprise.

FINDING: THE QUEST FOR HOMECOMING

2.1 *The Return*

"Finding" suggests a relentless forward movement until one finds what one is looking for. And some people make this the major theme of life itself: ever onward and ever forward!

But in order to find, a person may need to go back to the starting point, for it is easy to get side-tracked or lose our way in our seeking. In the spiritual journey, one's growth is not an accumulative process along straight lines. Rather, conversion and repentance remain part of the journey. This is the call to return.

Meister Eckhart points to the dynamic nature of grace in this regard. He writes, "Grace is not a stationary thing; it is always found in a Becoming."[1] Grace brings the new into being. Grace sculpts us. But grace not only calls us forward, but also backward: to our waywardness, our wounding, our lack of forgiveness. Thus Eckhart invites us to "find God where you have lost him."[2]

This calls us back to the beginning of our faith journey, where we acknowledge our lostness and embrace the grace of God in Christ for our healing and homecoming. But this move may be tumultuous, for we are often tugged between the pull of grace and the vice of our own resistance. St. Augustine describes this tension: "I sighed, and thou didst hear me. I vacillated and thou guided me. I roamed the broad way of the world, and thou didst not desert me."³ Here we see the tension between our will and God's good desire for us. In this wrestling, we are called to trust the triumph of grace, even as we confess our desperate need for God. As Augustine writes, "The true good of every created thing is always to cleave fast to thee, lest, in turning away from thee, it loses the light it had received."⁴

This turning and finding must be a re-occurring theme in the Christian life. For having been found, we continue to lose our way. Discouragement, unfaithfulness, tragedy may well come our way. Doubt ever lurks within us, and going our own way so easily displaces God's call and purposes.

We cannot ignore or run away from these things. For, as one of the Desert Fathers reminds us, "If a trial comes upon you in the place where you live do not leave that place… wherever you go, you will find that what you are running from is ahead of you."⁵ Thus we need to return. We need to face things—not in flight, but in the light of God's grace. The English mystic, Julian of Norwich, writes, "He [God] shows us our sin so quietly, and then we are sorry…we turn to see his mercy and cling to his love and goodness for we realize that he is our medicine."⁶

Having confessed, we move forward once again—not in our own strength, but by clinging to God and trusting him to carry us forward. By having made the return, by going back to face our issues, we move forward in a different way, for humility now marks us. Our gait is slower. We are more reflective. We move as contemplatives into action, not as activists rushing ahead with our own ideas and projects.

Having found grace at the point of our return—and not the condemnation and rejection we feared—we are more generous to ourselves and also to others. Grace, rather than judgement, marks all we do.

Reflection

St. Bernard of Clairvaux says it well:
"Let him [her] mourn, but not without holy
love and in hope of consolation."[7]

2.2 *Self-Knowledge*

The spiritual journey is not simply the quest to find God, for it also has to do with finding oneself. St. Isaac the Syrian, the seventh-century ascetic writer, writes: "He [she] who sees oneself as he [she] is, is greater than the one who raises the dead."[8] His point is that the exercise of spiritual gifts and powers must be rooted in self-insight. Put more pointedly, the gifts of God must be nestled in the grace of God, and spiritual power must be framed in a virtuous life. The first question is not what you do, but what motivates you.

However, as we find God, we simultaneously find ourselves. As St. Augustine says, "O eternal God, could I but know who I am and who thou art."[9] Yet the discovery of the self does not automatically lead to God, for it may lead to narcissism or despair. St. Anselm grieves, "If I look within myself, I cannot bear myself." At the same time, he recognizes, "If I do not look within myself, I do not know myself."[10]

The knowledge of the self in isolation or the knowledge of the self turned in on itself leads to a distorted self-knowledge. Finding ourselves is never a matter of endless inner excavations, for we can mine ourselves to death! Nor do we endlessly re-create ourselves, for we have to embrace our heritage and history, even as we develop and grow personally. We must embrace who we are, but who we are now is not the end of the story. Instead, we lean expectantly towards who we might yet become.

We must discover who we are in relationship, in the face of others. In Christian spirituality, this includes the discovery of ourselves in the light of the Great Other. St. Francis, lover of Christ and lover of the created world, says, "What a person is before God, that he [she] is and no more."[11]

This discovery of who I am in the face of God is a healing discovery. In this "homecoming," I realize that I am known and loved. I come to see God's great redemptive action in Christ towards me. I receive the welcome gift of the Spirit. Thus I am not only known and loved, I am also forgiven and empowered. To live out of this forgiveness, rather than my own demands, is a joy-filled life.

This life of joy shapes me in the likeness of Christ, an on-going journey in greater and greater conformity to the Way of Christ. St. Columbanus, the great Irish missionary to Europe, implies an attitude of humility and receptiveness in this process: "Let Christ paint his own image in us."[12] Created by the God who called all things into being, we are re-shaped by God's creative activity through the renewing work of the Spirit.

Thus in finding ourselves, we are called away from self-creation and invited into a dynamic love relationship with the God who does not overwhelm us, but invites into graced cooperation with all that God seeks to do in us and through us.

Reflection

The unknown author of *The Cloud of Unknowing* describes this cooperation as follows:
"That which I am and the way that I am,
with all my gifts of nature and grace,
you have given to me, O Lord,
and you are all of this.
I offer it all to you,
principally to praise you
and to help my fellow Christians and myself."[13]

FINDING: THE QUEST FOR HOMECOMING

2.3 *Finding One's Vocation*

It is one thing to find God and to know oneself, but it is also important to discover one's vocation in life. This is not to suggest that we only ever have one job. We may have many, but these should express our giftedness and God's calling.

In the history of Christian spirituality, there have been emphases that seem to call us away from concern with daily affairs and the "work-a-day" world. Thomas à Kempis reflects on this in *The Imitation of Christ*: "Live as becomes a pilgrim and stranger on earth, unconcerned about the world's cares, and keep your heart free and raised to God, for this earth of ours is no lasting city."[14]

Yet it is also possible to be fully engaged in daily work and the issues of our time while living this "pilgrim" life as an inner disposition. We can be committed to a world-formative Christianity while also being contemplative. For the fruit of contemplation can guide and shape our action.

As Geert de Groote writes, we need to do more than pray, for "labour is necessary for the well-being of mankind."[15] Thus we have a calling to be engaged with our world through our daily work and use our giftedness and resources, express our creativity, provide for those for whom we have responsibility, and contribute to the common good in our society. For "we shall be judged for the evil we have done, but especially for the good we have neglected and for the fact that we have not loved our neighbour," writes St. Maximus the Confessor (c.580–662), Abbot at the monastery at Chrysopolis.[16]

We will each have to wrestle with the question of our particular vocation. God is unlikely to send a postcard with the message: become a doctor or a priest. For as the unknown author of *The Cloud of Unknowing* points out, "God, the Lord of nature, will never anticipate man's [woman's] choices which follow one after another in time."[17] Put in more contemporary terms: God does not treat us as pre-programmed robots. Instead, God gives us freedom to make life choices. But these choices should always be made within the frame of God's biblical narrative of salvation, healing, responsibility and calling.

Yet as St. Catherine of Genoa warns us, so often "we end up doing our own will under many covers—of charity, of necessity or of justice."[18] So how may we know God's will? One guiding concept is that God uses our own life journey. The Desert Father, Anthony, reveals: "The Fathers of old went forth into the desert and when [they] themselves were made whole, they became physicians, and returning again they made others whole."[19] In other words, the goodness they received from God shaped their work and ministry.

Another guiding principle in our discernment is to seek to live and work in faithfulness to the life of Jesus. Gregory of Nyssa (c.330–395), Bishop of Nyssa and a great theologian and orator, points out: "Those who have an equal zeal for the good must thoroughly imitate and follow the pioneer of our salvation, and must put into practice what he has shown them."[20] A missionary is called to minister to others in the way of Jesus. What this means for a farmer or an engineer who is a Christian will always be a challenge. But to follow Jesus means to love God and neighbour, to be a healing and peace-making presence in the world and to have a heart for the poor.

Reflection

Within the contours of the quest for the good,
Meister Eckhart's advice is helpful:
"God does not look at what you
do, but only at your love… [God] does
care a lot about the attitudes our deeds express."[21]

2.4 *Being Found*

With our contemporary emphasis on being self-made persons, we have little sense of what others have done for us and the way they have sculpted and enriched our lives. We also have little sense that in the journey towards greater self-insight, others play an important role. Thus, seeing ourselves as self-made, we are hardly characterized by gratitude.

In this regard, we need only think of what family and friends can see in us that we don't recognize in ourselves, both good and bad. Furthermore, close and significant relationships can call forth in us what we did not know was there. And life in some form of intentional community can be the school of vulnerability, insight and growth.

But life's crises and difficulties can also draw out some of our worse or better qualities. The Early Church Father Origen (c.185–c.254) notes: "Temptations…serve the purpose of showing us who we really are."[22] Evagrius (346–399), a monk and spiritual writer, says similarly: "Many passions are hidden in our soul, but escape our attention. It is a sudden temptation which reveals them."[23] Temptations are thus an invitation to self-reflection, not self-recrimination or blame.

As a consequence, the journey of life is not simply about finding ourselves, but also about being found—by God, by others and through life's difficulties. This melody line calls us to be attentive, open and vulnerable to the voice of God and others through our life circumstances. As Bonaventure (1221–1274), theologian and Minister General of the Franciscan Order, suggests, "Open your eyes, alert the ears of your spirit. Open your lips and apply your heart so that in all creatures you may see, hear, praise, love and worship, glorify and honour your God."[24]

While others can "find" us, God seeks us out because God loves and is seeking to restore all of creation. God sees us as precious but lost, valued but flawed, graced but disobedient. God sees our wanderings and seeks to bring us home into the circle of Trinitarian love. St. Bernard of Clairvaux writes, "Every soul among you that is seeking God will know that he has gone before and sought you before you sought him."[25]

There are many dimensions to being found by God, for no one comes to faith in a pre-described way. While being found may involve our own seeking or the witness of others, God reaches out to us through his Word and Spirit. In this encounter we stop running, come to our senses and are turned around. And we begin to understand most clearly, as a personal revelation, God's healing love in Christ.

This is the good news of the gospel of Christ. This news is not first and foremost about what we must do, but what God has already provided in drawing us into the salvation that makes us whole.

Being found is not a reflection on our own lack of dignity or resolve, it is simply a recognition that we cannot save ourselves. But help has been waiting since before we were born. The cup was already full—we only need to come and drink.

Reflection

The words of Thomas à Kempis speak of
this spiritual homecoming dynamic:
"I [Jesus] have come because you have invited me.
Your tears and yearnings of your soul,
together with your humility and contrite heart,
have moved Me and brought you to Me."[26]

2.5 *Not-Finding*

There is something extremely worrying about people who make the claim that they know exactly who God is, how God works in the world, and what God is doing in their or other people's lives. While this may inspire a sense of absolute certainty in our precarious existence, this way of understanding the faith is less than helpful. This way of relating to God is more about control than a deep trust in the God who is ahead of us.

For we live the Christian life by faith, not certainty. And while we believe that God has revealed himself in the Word and the church, in nature and in life's circumstances, this revelation can only be accepted in faith and humility. Furthermore, the creature can hardly claim to fully understand the Creator. As Richard Rolle writes, "God is truly of infinite greatness, better than we think."[27] Or, as St. Anselm acknowledges, "I only saw you in a certain degree and not as you are."[28]

Our understanding of God is not only partial, but also one-sided, because we picture God in terms of our personal experience, our church formation and in the light of our culture. While in earlier times God was seen as the Great King, in our day we see God as a Friendly Helper. Julian of Norwich reflects on this one-sided way of seeing God: "For of all the good things our minds can think about God, it is thinking upon his goodness that pleases him the most and brings the most profit to our soul."[29] Yet we also need to see God as the one who forgives, heals, and reprimands us. While it is right to see God as Friend, we also need to see God as Lord. While God is the one who gives, God also calls us into his purposes. God calls us into grace, but also into meaningful work.

As we acknowledge our human limitations and wrestle with these tensions, we live into the mystery, rather than the certainty, of faith. For certainty can so easily lead to dogmatism, which can lead to arrogance—which produces judgementalism. This is the ugly face of religiosity. But living in the mystery of faith implies humility. This does not mean that we don't know God, but that God knows us far more than we know ourselves.

Meister Eckhart notes that God "is a hidden God," and "the more one seeks Thee, the less one can find Thee."[30] This sounds counter-intuitive. Surely, the more one seeks, the more one can find. And having found, one has. And having, one possesses. And what one possesses, one controls.

But not so with God! The more one seeks to control God, the more God withdraws. For we do not seek after God to possess God, but to be found by God. If we are to be known by God, we must learn to know and love God in the darkness as well as the light. Meister Eckhart invites us to consider the following: "When you are in low condition and feel forsaken see if you are just as true to him [God] as when your sense of him is most vivid and if you act the same when you think all help and comfort [is] far removed as you do when God seems nearest."[31] The darkest place may not necessarily be the most dismal. It is there that our sense of mystery may burst into blossom.

Reflection

The movement of the Christian life is not
simply from the darkness of sin
to the light of God's salvation in Christ.
It is also a movement from the light of
Christ into the greater mystery of God's Spirit.

3

JOURNEYING:
Spiritual Pilgrimage

It can be said that the Christian is on an upward journey to God, an inner journey of spirituality and an outward journey of service to the world. Everything about the Christian life thus has to do with journeying. We come home in faith to the welcoming heart of God, but we also seek to grow more deeply in the love of God, thus continuing our journey towards God. We are invited to journey through life towards God's great final future, thus we are journeying towards heaven.

And we are also invited to journey more deeply into the world and the issues of our time.

There are some key dimensions to being the journeying people of God in the world, or in the words of the Vatican II documents, being God's pilgrim people.

The first and most obvious is that we are sojourners, not settlers. And to use the imagery of the Old Testament, we are God's tabernacle rather than God's temple people. Being unsettled is not always psychologically easy, but it keeps us from stagnation.

JOURNEYING: SPIRITUAL PILGRIMAGE

And living this way means that we remain open to the Spirit as we seek to do the will of God by finding God's purpose for our lives—even if it means radical relinquishment, downward mobility or relocating for the sake of the gospel.

Another consequence of being God's pilgrim people is that we are not overly embedded in the values of our culture. A person on pilgrimage is present in the world, but also disconnected. This reflects our in-the-world, but not of-the-world status as the people of God. And this can provide us with a different way of seeing, because we have a different way of being in the world. Paul puts this in the clearest terms: "Let those who have wives be as though they had none, and those who mourn as though they were not mourning, and those who buy as though they had no possessions, and those who deal with the world as though they had no dealings with it. For the present form of the world is passing away" (1 Corinthians 7:29–31). This is not an invitation to abandon the world, but rather to engage it from a very different perspective. In this invitation, we embrace a radical "disconnect" so that a radical re-connection may take place for the sake of the gospel and the Reign of God.

Peter also picks up this theme when he writes, "Beloved, I urge you as aliens and exiles to abstain from the desires of the flesh that wage war against the soul. Conduct yourselves honorably among the gentiles, so that, though they malign you as evildoers, they may see your honorable deeds" (1 Peter 2:11–12). Thus by being different, the people of God may be a light to the world.

Our journey towards God, rather than moving us away from the issues of our time, throws us more deeply into the world as a healing and renewing presence. Thus our inner journeys of prayer and reflection must give glory to God and sustain us in our service to the world.

JOURNEYING: SPIRITUAL PILGRIMAGE

3.1 *The Journey Towards God*

For some, we only journey towards God when we surrender and convert to faith in God. Yet the Christian life is an ongoing journey, through communion and prayer, towards the God who has already found us. For God is not simply an instrument to make us well, but the very ground of our being.

St. Augustine hints at the journeying status of the Christian when he speaks about "holy angels, who enjoy uninterrupted happiness" in the presence of God, "render[ing] assistance" to us who are "still wandering."[1] This church father is not referring to the Christian's "wandering" as an act of disobedience or indifference, but is describing our fundamental status as pilgrims, reminding us that we need God's companionship and provision of bread for the journey of faith.

In this pilgrimage of faith, we are journeying towards the God who is already with us. This is a journey we are all called to make. And it is a journey where we are called to deepen our relationship with God. The reasons for this are manifold. The New Testament is clear that we are called to grow in Christian maturity (Ephesians 4:15–16) and Christ-likeness (1 Corinthians 11:1). In this journey we are to be rooted in the community of faith (Ephesians 4:11–13), and we are called to a life of worship (Revelation 7:15), prayer (Romans 12:12) and service (Galatians 6:10).

But this is no easy journey. Instead, it is challenging, convoluted, and sometimes brutal. The reasons for this are complex. We are with God, but there are also headwinds. We are safe with God, but not yet fully healed. We are in the Kingdom of God, but the Kingdom is not yet fully in us or in our world. We are people of prayer, but we are also wayward. We love God, but we are also self-preoccupied. We want to go God's way, but we are also disobedient.

Consequently, the journey towards God is not a smooth, straight line. We sometimes lose our way. We are tempted and give in. And much of what we seek to do to the glory of God and in the service of others is often so skimpy and broken.

Thomas à Kempis is right when he says, "As long as there is anything that holds me down, I cannot freely fly to You."[2] And there is much that holds us down. Most often what sidetracks us is that we still think that we know best. We find it hard to believe that God's way is best for us and others—and fully trusting God is difficult for us.

St. Ambrose makes a related point: "You received Him into the dwelling of your mind; you saw Him in [the] spirit; you saw with inner eyes. Hold fast your new Guest, long awaited but lately received."[3] Indeed, hold God fast! And grow into an ever deeper relationship!

JOURNEYING: SPIRITUAL PILGRIMAGE

The journey towards God is not easy, but we are called to walk along this way in faith. Clearly, God's Spirit needs to sustain us. Clearly, we need to find a new humility. Clearly, we need to discover a deeper communion. Clearly, we need to discover a deeper trust in the God who walks this way with us.

Reflection

St. Augustine speaks about this trust:
"But see, O Lord, we are thy little flock.
Possess us.
Stretch thy wings above us.
And let us take refuge under them.
Be thou our glory; let us be loved for thy sake."[4]

3.2 *The Imitatio Christi*

Christ has been sculpted in many differing images: the conquering king, the suffering servant, the other-worldly Palestinian peasant, the social revolutionary, the pacifist, and so on.

But we are not following the Christ of our own making, who would be easy to follow. Rather, we are invited to follow the Christ of the gospel story and the Pauline epistles, and not to play off the one set of writings against the other. But this poses a challenge for us. It is one thing to embrace the Christ of the gospels, who shows compassion, heals people, serves the poor and confronts the bigotry of the religious establishment of his day. It is quite something else to embrace the Christ who is glorified and who holds all things together: "He himself is before all things, and in him all things hold together" (Colossians 1:17).

Clearly, while we in faith can embrace Christ in his humanity and divinity, following him and being like him is usually cast in terms of what we see in his earthly ministry. St. Francis points us in this direction: "Inwardly cleansed, interiorly enlightened and inflamed by the fire of the Holy Spirit, may we be able to follow in the footsteps of Your beloved Son."[5] But St. Francis' language is important. This is no automatic following, for it requires our inner purgation and empowerment. And it is cast as a prayer: God help us so that we may be able to follow in this way.

St. Clare initially casts our following of Christ in similar terms: "By following in his [Christ's] footsteps of poverty and humility, you can always carry him spiritually in your body," but then she broadens this out: "And you will hold him by whom you and all things are held together."[6] She joins the gospel vision with the Pauline vision of the one we are to follow.

One way to understand this is that the following of Christ and the *imitatio Christi* is not simply about preaching, healing, praying or serving in the way Christ did, with an emphasis on external conformity. Something much deeper is at play here. Christ is being formed in us. This is a Christo-mystic reality, where witness and service flow from an inner spirituality, rather than an outward conformity.

This opens wide possibilities, for the *imitatio Christi* is no longer simply the domain of the missionary, but the scope of the whole people of God in bearing Christ into the world—the business person, the scientist, the politician. All are called to pray, to bring good news, to be a healing presence, to push back the powers of darkness, to resist legalistic spirituality, to bring shalom and goodness into our world.

To be the followers of Christ and to be like Christ is no narrow calling. This calling might mean being an exorcist, preacher, prophet, and healer, yet its scope is the mending of all creation and the restoration of all things. As we live out this calling, we participate in the new humanity of which Christ is the New Adam, and we envision a new order dancing in the restorative grace of God.

As we both follow and become like Christ, the reign of God springs up in our neighbourhoods, the places where we work and in the economic and political spheres of life, illuminating everything with an inner spirituality that nurtures a life of witness and brings about human flourishing to the glory of God.

Reflection

St. Cyril of Alexandria points us in this direction:
"Christ is for us
a pattern and image of the divine way of life,
and he displayed clearly
how and in what manner
it is fitting for us to live."[7]

3.3 *Many Journeys*

Conservative Christians tend to get nervous around the notion of diversity. In order to feel safe and secure they hold tight to the idea that there is only *one* way. After all, Jesus proclaimed, "I am the way, and the truth and the life" (John 14:6).

But one can uphold Jesus as the true source of salvation and life and still acknowledge that there are multiple ways in which the life-giving work of Christ through the Spirit unfolds in people's lives. The English Christian mystic, Richard Rolle, writes: "There is one righteousness and many paths by which we are led to the joy of life everlasting."[8] How exciting and freeing this is!

This means, amongst other things, that there is no singular path of conversion. There is not one way to pray. There is no predictable path in Christian growth. God does not engage each of us in exactly the same way. How wonderful! How liberating! How deeply personal!

This also has some important implications. The first is that God does not work in stereotypical ways. God does not have a one-dance routine. Job touches on this: "He [God] does great things and unsearchable, marvelous things without number" (Job 5:9). God works in myriad ways.

Second, God works in a profoundly relational way. God does not respond to us out of a program or strategy, but personally, out of love. Meister Eckhart highlights this: "God does not work in all hearts alike but according to the preparation and sensitivity he finds in each."[9] This highlights a profound relational dynamic. God works with what is within us right where we are. God does not violate us. God uniquely births us into new life.

This is revealed in the very differing conversion accounts of Paul and Timothy. Paul's conversion was confrontative, almost over-powering in its revelatory light (Acts 9:3–5). By contrast, Timothy's was a gentle, familial unfolding (2 Timothy 1:5). Paul's was a summer storm, Timothy's a gentle sunrise. Every conversion is God working in each individual.

God's wonderfully diverse way of working in us is also revealed through the diversity of gifts and callings that the Spirit pours out on the community of faith. Some teach; others are healers; some are prophets; some have the gifts of generosity and hospitality (Romans 12:6–8; 1 Corinthians 12:4–11; Ephesians 4:11–12). God empowers us all differently.

In this diversity of gifts and callings, we must not elevate one gift over another nor judge others in the light of the gifts and callings we have received, as if we have become the standard. Here the words of the Desert Father, Abbot Pastor, are insightful: "If there be three in one place and one of them lives the life of holy quiet, and another is ill and gives thanks, and the third tends them with an honest heart, these three are alike, as if their work was one."[10]

Yet all too readily, we elevate the achiever over the doer, the priest over the laity, the successful person over the struggler. We have little sense that the small way is the royal road.

The challenge for all of us in contemporary global Christianity is to recognize gender and cultural differences in understanding and expressing the faith we have in Christ. Moreover, we need to acknowledge the differing stages of life as one seeks to live in fidelity to the gospel in the vigour of youth and through the challenges of family and work and in one's old age.

And in all of this, we need to see the wide sweep of God's work while at the same time being secure in the God who makes the swallow dwell securely in God's holy place (Psalm 84:3).

Reflection

John Cassian reminds us:
"One prays another way when the life of
the Spirit is flourishing,
and another when pushed down by the
mass of temptation."[11]

3.4 *Seeking Our Own Pathways*

Though we are on an ongoing journey towards God, an inner journey to deeper attentiveness to the Spirit moving within us, and an outward journey of love and service to our neighbours, our pathways are marked by many blockages. We move forward, but there is resistance. We journey, yet become discouraged. We know what we must do, yet we lose our way. In terms forged by Martin Luther, we continue to be sinner-saints.

What this highlights is that no part of the journey is a breeze—not even when we are in the midst of revival or renewal. No part of the journey is without its challenges. Therefore, we don't graduate from one level to another. No one ascends the ladder of the Christian journey to a state of full sanctity. With St. Patrick (c.389–c.461), the apostle to the Irish, we can all say, "I have nothing of value that is not his great gift."[12] As a consequence, all language of progress is unhelpful, such as the language of Jan van Ruysbroeck (1293–1381), the Flemish mystic who distinguishes "faithful servants" from the "inward friends of God," with the latter being in a higher state of grace.[13] In fact, this should be turned around! We become friends of God and so become faithful servants.

JOURNEYING: SPIRITUAL PILGRIMAGE

Since the journey of faith is no picnic and there are many blockages and temptations along the way, we might ask, what is our most enduring difficulty? Our greatest challenge is neither dishonesty nor selfishness, nor our many petty and stupid wrongdoings. If we make the painful inner journey of self-insight, we will discover that much deeper, at the base of our human condition is our on-going self-willfulness.

Spawned in our primeval beginnings, at the core of our humanity, this self-assertion seeks to set aside God's way. As a consequence, as St. Anselm points out, "[We] lost the blessedness for which we were made, and found the wretchedness for which we were not made."[14]

This core feature of the human condition expresses itself in a foolishness that is self-harming. The weeping prophet of Israel understood this only too well: "For my people have committed two evils: they have forsaken me, the fountain of living water, and have dug cisterns for themselves, cracked cisterns that can hold no water" (Jeremiah 2:13). Thus our waywardness not only moves us away from God, but also creates substitutes that are death-dealing rather than life-giving.

St. Catherine of Siena (1347–1380), a Dominican tertiary and mystic, picks up this theme under a different analogy: "How foolish and blind are those who choose to cross through the water when the road has been built for them."[15] Indeed, how often we go our own burdensome way rather than walking in the lightness of God's sustaining way for us!

In the language of Christian spirituality, we often speak of the need for a change of heart, yet we would do better to speak of a transformation of our will. The volitional core of who we are needs the transforming work of the Spirit so that we will the "one thing needful," in the words of Soren Kierkegaard, which is to will what God wants and asks of us, even if that is akin to Abraham's call to sacrifice his son (Genesis 22:1–14).

This calls us to die to our old selves—in openness, humility and docility—and to be shaped anew by Christ through the renewing power of the Spirit of God.

Reflection

Thomas à Kempis reminds us:
"If you should throw off one cross
you will surely find another and perhaps one
that is even heavier."[16]

JOURNEYING: SPIRITUAL PILGRIMAGE

3.5 *Provisions on the Journey*

Our contemporary way of life is framed by the age of anxiety. Many people are fearful about their personal safety and security. Society in general feels unsafe. Our neighbourhoods and places of work no longer feel safe. Even our homes are places of fear, with relationship breakdown and various forms of abuse.

This anxiety has made us wary of strangers and skeptical about the leaders of our political and social institutions. For many, even the church—supposedly the "communion of saints"— has become suspect.

One understandable but unfortunate response to all this anxiety has been to become more self-focused and self-protective. Societally, we have attempted to put more regulations in place to sustain something of the common good in the face of a lack of trust and community.

Clearly, we need a social revolution that recaptures openness to others—even strangers. We need to rebuild our human communities with the oil of trust. We need to discover anew the joy of working for the common good rather than for narrow personal and tribal interests.

This revolution is first and foremost a revolution of the heart. And it is inaugurated within us when we discover that we are loved beyond our achievements, we are safe in being found, we are known in the secret places of our being, we are accompanied in our loneliness, and we are empowered in all the good we seek to do. This is the music of the God who accompanies us in all the contours of life's journey.

Through this way of being in the world, we may discover that in the seeming unlikely places, goodness appears. In the words of the Ambrosian Acclamations: "O bread eternal, you feed the hunger of your people in desert places."[17]

This resonates with the great Old Testament prophetic tradition, as we see in Isaiah's vision: "I am about to do a new thing; now it springs forth, do you not perceive it? I will make a way in the wilderness and rivers in the desert" (Isaiah 43:19). The Psalmist also picks up this theme: "As they go through the valley of Baca they make it a place of springs; the early rain also covers it with pools" (Psalm 84:6).

Here we touch on desert spirituality, a Christian tradition that speaks about stumbling on to grace and goodness in places of desolation. For God is not simply in the expected places of the sanctuary or piety. But in the dry places of our lives, God can cause a river to flow. This does not convey God's unpredictability, but rather highlights God's love and presence in the good and difficult places of our lives.

God can sustain us in difficult places through family, friends and the goodness and generosity of others, but most profoundly through his mysterious presence. This inner sustenance is the work of the Spirit generating hope and life. And no matter how desolate the circumstances or the inner chambers of the heart, it is possible to join with St. Patrick in saying: "I arise today through God's strength to pilot me; God's might to uphold me; God's wisdom to guide me."[18]

This does not mean that God only rescues us, but rather that God is with us, nourishing and sustaining us—even in desolate places.

Reflection

Theophilus (died 412), Patriarch of Alexandria, proclaims:
"Eat the bread which purges away the old bitterness,
and drink the wine
which eases the pain of the wound."[19]

4

WONDERING:
The Gift of a Child-like Faith

I have been part of the life of the church for all of my life and have participated in various church fellowships in Australia, Asia and North America. This certainly does not give me a birds-eye view of what is happening in the wider church, but I have gained a particular impression—that as church, we don't live with a sense of wonderment.

A few possibilities for why this is so come to mind. First, the church has traditionally marketed itself as an institution of certainty: sure about who God is, sure about what God does, adamant that it has the right interpretation of the Bible. It claims that it has over 2000 years of history on its side in case of the Roman Catholic Church and over 500 years if one is a Protestant. Certainties are found in the church's traditions, structures, theology, liturgies, practices and its spirituality.

Secondly, the way the church operates militates against the notion of wonderment. We have teachers and preachers, priests and pastors who function in a framework where there is no space for interaction, let alone dialogue or reflection. And while in liturgical churches there is the space for wonderment around the Eucharistic celebration—a dimension sadly lacking in many Protestant churches—even this element of the service is constrained by the framework of words and the pressure to keep within time limits. If wonderment needs quiet and reflective spaces—and it does—then church has little time for a such a luxury.

Thirdly, the whole mission of the church is premised on the fact that it has a clear-cut task and word for the world. The church must therefore be confident in its proclamation and witness if it is to be effective.

While these things are true, they are not the whole story. And the other part of the story has nothing to do with being confused, vague, hesitant, irrelevant and inward-focused. Nor does it have anything to do with dumbing-down or reducing the richness of the Christian story to generalities like simply being a nice person.

What I am leaning towards is a rejection of stridency, on the one hand, and an insipid niceness on the other. One can be a deeply grounded Christian believer and still be marked by a child-like simplicity of heart. One can be steeped in theology and still live with a sense of wonder. One can be committed to one's faith and still have a great openness to people of other faiths. One can be sure and still have questions. One can have faith and still live in hope. One can be knowledgeable and still embrace mystery.

There is something wonderfully disarming about a person who dreams and who is marked with a sense of wonder. I have often seen this beauty in my ten-year-old granddaughter, Bronte, who after school can play for hours on our back deck, lost in the wonder of a self-created game imitating the butterflies that flit on the outer edges of the mighty tuckeroo tree that graces our backyard. I don't see this gift in myself, nor in most Christians I know. We are pragmatic and functional. We are as busy as anyone else. And we seldom breathe the air of a joyful spirit and a sense of wonder about God and his world. Maybe St. Francis is calling us?

4.1 Finding Francis, Finding Wonderment

Most people experience Christianity as a rather somber religion. Some of the key tenets of its faith focus on sin, the death of Christ, confession, overcoming our deep-seated flaws, costly service and a life of relinquishment. In a world that celebrates self-fulfillment, much-having, freedom and pleasure, the above scenario is a public relations disaster. Little wonder that many people, particularly in the West, no longer find Christianity all that attractive.

While there are churches that are more entertainment-oriented and some churches that give a healthy place to the use of art in worship, generally speaking, our church services are not particularly stimulating or life-giving events. So we should not be surprised that many Christians no longer darken the doors of our sanctuaries.

But the Christian faith is a religion of joy: the joy of salvation, friendship with God, the blessing of healing, the creative inspiration of the Spirit, grateful worship, the joyful challenge of serving God in our world, the inspiration of dreams, the fruit of contemplation. St. Francis of Assisi, an iconic person in the history of Christianity, reflects this joy-filled way of living the Christian life. We turn to him for inspiration, for we need to discover the joy of God, and our eyes need to be filled with wonder once again.

IN THE FOOTSTEPS

St. Francis was much more than a lover of birds. He was deeply changed by Christ, and he sought to live the gospel, re-build the church, serve the poor and befriend the Muslims of his day. Francis speaks about being "inwardly cleansed, interiorly enlightened, and inflamed by the fire of the Holy Spirit" so that we are "able to follow in the footsteps of [God's] beloved Son."[1] And he goes on to say that we are called "to observe the holy Gospel of our Lord Jesus Christ, living in obedience without personal possessions and in chastity."[2] There is nothing flippant about this radical call, yet Francis was a man of joy and wonderment. He loved God. He loved humanity. He loved the poor. He loved all that God has made.

Bonaventure, in writing about St. Francis, notes: "When he pronounced or heard the name 'Jesus' he was filled with joy interiorly and seemed to be altered exteriorly."[3] But more than this, he was full of wonder. Bonaventure recounts: "With a feeling of unprecedented devotion he savored in each and every creature—as in many rivulets—that Goodness which is their fountain-source."[4]

Along with Francis, may Jesus become a joy for us and not simply a responsibility. May prayer become a place of wonder rather than a duty. May all people be seen as friends and not simply as strangers. May the Gospel be seen as inspiration and not simply as guide. May service be seen as grace and not simply as task. May the whole created world be seen with the eyes of love and not simply in terms of acquisition and exploitation.

This calls us to radical inner surgery and a whole new way of being. In the words of Jacopone da Todi (1236–1306), the great Italian Franciscan poet, "Let the ice in you begin to thaw. And your heart rejoice in new found riches."[5]

While we are always called to witness and service through the grace of God, we are also invited to wonder and to dream. To wonder anew, we will need to recover Joel's prophetic vision: "I will pour out my spirit on all flesh; your sons and your daughters shall prophesy, your old men shall dream dreams, and your young men shall see visions" (Joel 2:28).

Reflection

In the words of St. Anselm:
"Admit me into the inner room of your love"
and there may I
"be completely held in your care."[6]

4.2 *To Wonder and Not Be Afraid*

When we wonder, we are overcome with awe and amazement. We marvel at something—a flash of beauty, an inspirational moment, an incredible event of nature—that comes unexpectedly, as a surprise. Yet amidst daily life and relationships, we also wonder about what is going on in our family or the workplace, when the more normal and predictable ways of functioning seem to be disturbed. We wonder about people's actions. We wonder what people mean by the things they are saying. We wonder what is really going on around us. This is an interior questioning, as we try to make sense of something that is neither clear nor obvious.

While the first meaning of "wonder" has to do with a sudden and unexpected burst of awe, the second has more to do with a sense of unease and even suspicion. In the former, we are overcome by something beyond us; in the latter, we are in control.

But to wonder can also mean to muse, speculate or ruminate. The medieval Christian mystical writer and Scottish monastic, Richard of St. Victor (died 1173), opens up this contemplative dimension when he writes, "Wonder takes its beginning when we discern something beyond hope and above expectation."[7]

WONDERING: THE GIFT OF A CHILD-LIKE FAITH

If hope lies in the future, then wonder resides in the domain of the present, where the future hope is felt and believed to be alluringly near at hand, faintly visible, but not yet fully apprehended. Thus while I may say that I hope that God will do something to remedy a problem or situation, I can't quite say the same about wonder. For since musing brings together awe and speculation, there is an immediacy about wondering. The wonder of Christmas is neither past nor future: it is present.

When we are filled with wonder, the wonder of God comes near. This is what we long for, yet is so often missing, in our contemporary Christianity. Devoid of awe and wonder, we have domesticated God, relegating God's presence to the sidelines of our existence and imagination. We have turned the fiery nature of the young stallion into a tired donkey. Our imaginations have become old and outworn with dogma.

We desperately need to breathe, long, and anticipate again. St. Bernard of Clairvaux points us in the right direction when he writes, "Freed from the heavy burden of my own will, I may breathe freely under the light load of [God's] love."[8] Richard Rolle says something similar when he prays that his "mind…may swiftly flee into the high mirth of love."[9] And Jan van Ruysbroeck is even more explicit: "All our powers then fail us and we fall down in open contemplation. All becomes one and one becomes all in the living embrace of the three-fold Unity. When we experience this Unity, we become one being, one life, and one blessedness with God."[10]

Wonder anticipates us. Wonder comes to us. And when it comes, it is never exhausted. We never cease to wonder.

When we wonder, we need to resist being afraid of our wonderings. We easily think that we may be wrong, that we hope for too much or that we are unrealistic. Thus we readily abandon our dreams. Instead, we should commit ourselves and all of our dreams and wonderings into the hands of God, as surely as Christ on the cross committed himself into his father's hands.

Reflection

And so we pray with St. Anselm:
"Refashion the face that I have spoiled,
restore the innocence that I have violated,"
so that I may live in the wonder of your love,
O my God and Redeemer.[11]

4.3 *The Beauty of the Lord*

When we think about God, we do not think initially of God's beauty, but of God's power, love, omnipresence, salvation, and so on. What we think about God reveals more about us than it does about God, for while God is wholly concerned with the whole creation, God is also wholly Other. Yet so often we cast God in purely functional and pragmatic terms, where God is defined by what God *does,* rather than who God *is*.

Our ancient forebears are quick to point out that knowing and loving God simply for what we can get back from God is a suspect love. St. Bernard of Clairvaux writes, "I am suspicious of a love in which there seems to be anything of a hope for gaining something."[12] Meister Eckhart adds, "If I have a friend and love him so that he may benefit me and do what I wish, then I do not love my friend at all but rather myself."[13] And Thomas à Kempis wisely directs us to consider that "a wise lover considers not so much the lover's gift as the giver's love. He [she] attends more to the giver's affection than to the gift's value."[14]

This challenge from Thomas à Kempis brings us to think about who God is and not simply about what God does. Although we know God through God's actions, we need to reflect on God's beauty as well as God's power.

Throughout the biblical narrative, the people of God marvel at who God is, particularly the psalmists: "One thing I asked of the Lord, that will I seek after: to live in the house of the Lord all the days of my life, to behold the beauty of the Lord, and to inquire in his temple" (Psalm 27:4). God's beauty evokes delight, and we are invited to "Take delight in the Lord, and he will give you the desires of your heart" (Psalm 37:4). The "beauty of the Lord" is connected to God's glory, which shines forth throughout the pages of scripture. God "is the King of glory" (Psalm 24:10). In Numbers, "the glory of the Lord appeared to the whole congregation" (16:19), and in Exodus Moses asked Yahweh to: "Show me your glory, I pray" (33:18). And Jesus describes the Lord's doing as "amazing in our eyes" (Matthew 21:42).

Our ancient forebears can show us the way back to this way of meditating on the glory of God. John Cassian (c.360–435), founder of several monasteries and a student of Egyptian monasticism, speaks of seeing the "magnificence of His creation" and the "spectacle of His justice," but also the "astonished gaze of His ungraspable nature."[15] Jan van Ruysbroeck reiterates this when he describes "one enjoyment and one beautitude with the Father in essential love."[16] And Meister Eckhart makes this clear: love God for "all that He himself is."[17]

The beauty of God is intrinsic to who God is. This beauty shines in the harmony and cooperation of Father, Son and Holy Spirit. This beauty is evident in the creation. This beauty manifests itself in God's healing and renewing power. In salvation, we are touched by the beauty of God.

Reflection

Bonaventure, in writing about St. Francis, notes:
"In beautiful things he saw beauty itself
and through the vestiges imprinted on creation
he followed his Beloved everywhere."[18]

4.4 *Participating in the Wonderful Works of God*

Some see God as irrelevant and totally removed from the issues of our time. Others see God as having a limited role in the world—namely, to save people and to prepare them for heaven. But others see God as intrinsic to our world and the whole universe—the Creator of all things, the One who sustains all things, and as the One who makes all things whole.

While St. Anselm makes this confession: "Jesus, good Lord, why did you come down from heaven [and] what did you do in the world…unless it was that you might save sinners,"[19] St. Augustine writes that God "has prepared for us the medicines of faith and applied them to the maladies of the whole world."[20] John Scottus Eriugena (c.810–c.877), the great Irish mystical theologian, also highlights God's purpose in restoring all things through Christ in his vision: the Word cried out invisibly to create the world, but "cried out visibly when he [Christ] came into the world to save it."[21] And Paul emphasized that through Christ, "God was pleased to reconcile to himself all things, whether on earth or in heaven, by making peace through the blood of his cross" (Colossians 1:20). Thus the salvation of God is personal, societal and cosmic. We are invited, through God's salvation in Christ, into the great restoration of all things, which will unite us and the earth and heaven once again.

WONDERING: THE GIFT OF A CHILD-LIKE FAITH

In this grand vision of the restoration of all things, we need to find our place—first as recipients of the grace and goodness of God and then as participants in the Spirit's renewing work in the world. We are called to faith and also to the mission of cooperating and joining with all that God is doing and seeking to do in the world. As equal partners with Christ, our Great Light, we point to him and let our flickering flame shine with passion and commitment. As St. Francis exhorts: "With our whole heart, our whole soul, our whole mind, with our whole strength and fortitude, with all our understanding, with all our powers, with every effort, every affection, every feeling, every desire and wish, let us love the Lord God."[22] And this love for God spills into the world of our families, neighbourhoods and workplaces.

St. Isaac the Syrian describes the vast scope of this love: "A heart aflame with love for the entire creation, for people, for birds, beasts, evil spirits, all creatures…[and] moved by an infinite pity that is awakened in the hearts of those who resemble God."[23] We are called to be the presence of God in every sphere of human endeavour and every dimension of life as we seek the restoration of all things—humans, nature, and all that is evil. There is no area of life over which the Lordship of Christ is not to be proclaimed.

This calling can only come from inner transformation through the Spirit and can only be sustained through the power of God, shaped by the wisdom of God, and borne into the world through the peace of Christ, for the blessing of others, to the glory of God.

Reflection

In this mission of the people of God in the world,
St. Cyril of Alexandria reminds us:
"Christ is for us a pattern and beginning
and image of the divine way of life,
and he displayed clearly how and in what
manner it is fitting for us to live."[24]

4.5 *The Communion of Saints*

In the West, our participation in the church is fraught with difficulties. Some Christians no longer attend worship services on a regular basis. Others have abandoned church all together. Many young people are ambivalent about this ancient institution. And scandals within church continue to attract bad press.

Yet we can't dismiss the church, for throughout the biblical story, it is clear that God builds a people. Jesus formed a common purse community, and from the Acts of the Apostles onward we see the emergence of house churches, where Christians met for worship, prayers, preaching and the eucharist.

Paul places a lot of emphasis on the importance of the faith community and calls it the body of Christ. Not only are we baptized into Christ (Romans 6:3), but we are also baptized into the body of Christ: "For in the one Spirit we were all baptized into one body—Jews or Greeks, slaves or free—and we were all made to drink of one Spirit" (1 Corinthians 12:13). In the pages of the New Testament the church is spoken about as a local gathering (1 Corinthians 1:2), the dwelling place of God's presence (1 Corinthians 3:9, 16), and a cosmic reality founded in the heart of God, which will come to completion in the ages to come (Colossians 1:15–20).

Thus the community of faith is full of mystery and is part of God's purposes for the restoration of all things. As forbearers of the new humanity in Christ, there is much to wonder about as we contemplate the church in its daily and ordinary reality and also what the church is in the heart of God and in the brooding presence of the Spirit. As God's eschatological community, the church is sent into the world to be a witness to all that God has done and is doing in the mending of all things (John 17:18). As contemplative and theologian William of St. Thierry (c.1085–c.1148) points out, "For to eat the body of Christ [in the eucharist] is nothing other than to be made the body of Christ and the temple of the Holy Spirit."[25]

The challenge facing Christians today is to acknowledge the ordinariness of the church and to live its mystery—a mystery that is rooted in God's redemptive activity. St. Anselm celebrates this: "By you [God] the world is renewed and made beautiful with truth, governed by the light of righteousness. By you sinful humanity is justified, the condemned are saved, the servants of sin and hell are set free."[26]

Thus the church is a community that enjoys God's healing activity. Christians are people who live in the forgiveness of Christ, experience the renewing presence of the Spirit and taste the powers of the future age (Hebrews 6:5). This is certainly not mundane! But it does challenge us to live out our faith. St. Ignatius (c.130–c.200), Bishop of Lyons, makes the point: "We have not only to be called Christians, but to be Christians."[27] And St. Benedict (c.480–c.550), the father of Western monasticism, describes what this means: "Your way of acting should be different from the world's way; the love of Christ must come before all else."[28] Saved through Christ, conformed to Christ, we are to be Christ in the world.

But we also need to live the communion of saints in the present, engaging in practical ecumenism, counter to the some 33,000 denominations that dot the landscape. In other words, we need to become neighbourhood churches praying and working together to be Christ's servants in the world.

Reflection

St. Cyprian (died 258), Bishop of Carthage, reminds us:
"The church, bathed in the light of the Lord,
spreads her rays throughout the world,
yet the light everywhere diffused is one light."[29]

5

CELEBRATING:
A Life of Gratitude

In spite of the massive entertainment industry in the West, Christians in the Majority World seem to know more about celebration than those in the Minority World (West). From my experiences in Australia and Asia, the West could be typified as a culture of complaint, while the Majority World could be described as a culture of hope. Much-having does not necessarily lead to happiness, for those who have little often live with joy.

As Christians, we respond to all that God has done for us with gratitude and thankfulness. We are grateful for the gifts of creation and for God's healing and renewing presence in our lives. Much has been given, thus thankfulness and celebration should mark the whole of our life's journey.

When we celebrate, we mark a special occasion—such as a birthday, a national event within our country, an achievement or milestone in life, the end of a war or other tragedy—with festivity and merriment, patterning that celebration into the fabric our lives. In the Christian calendar, we celebrate Christmas, Easter

CELEBRATING: A LIFE OF GRATITUDE

and the day of Pentecost—a feast we should celebrate even more, not only because the commercial world has not yet co-opted Pentecost, but also because the life-giving Spirit makes all that Christ is and has done real to us.

Festival celebrations characterized the people of the Old Testament (Leviticus 23). And in the New Testament, the Christian community celebrated by eating together and sharing the eucharist (Luke 22:14–20). Thus celebration is at the heart of our Christian life.

Following the monastic tradition, one way to celebrate the new life that Christ brings is to mark regular times in the day for contemplation and prayer. The Franciscan Daily Office, "Celebrating Daily Prayer," provides a rich tradition of reflection and celebration. We can also craft our own patterns and traditions as we pause in our day to stop and gaze, to think and pray, to rejoice and give thanks, and to celebrate all that is good in our lives and world. Celebration sustains us in our journeys through smooth and hard times, abundance and deprivation and certainty and deep questioning.

IN THE FOOTSTEPS

5.1 *Celebrating the Gift of Friendship*

It goes without saying that the way we relate and respond to others has much to do with the way we were treated in our early formation. When we are loved well for who we are, rather than for our achievements, we are shaped to love others with an openness and generosity of spirit.

In the realm of spirituality, when we know that we are loved well by the God of all grace, who embraces us even in our waywardness and folly, we are empowered to love others. St. Anselm speaks of this great friendship extended to us: "Jesus Christ, my dear and gracious Lord, you have shown a love greater than that of any man and which no one can equal, for you in no way deserved to die, yet you laid down your dear life for those who served you and sinned against you."[1] Living in the goodness of this kind of embrace, we are well placed to befriend others.

The friendship we receive and extend is one of the great gifts of life. Friendship is not predictable, but has the air of mystery. One can work hard on a relationship, yet it may never result in close bonding, while a casual encounter may grow into a friendship. Since we can't know ahead of time what may happen in our relationships, and since friendship is more than the application of certain strategies, friendship

CELEBRATING: A LIFE OF GRATITUDE

must be seen as a gift. Theologically, friendship may be seen as a small repetition of the mystery of the Trinity.

St. Ailred (Aelred, 1109–1167), the abbot of the monastic community of Rievaulx, offers a richly textured vision of friendship: "To converse and jest together, with good-will to honour one another, to read together, to discuss matters together, together to trifle and together to be in earnest; to differ at times without ill humour."[2] This spiritual father speaks of friendship in deeply human terms—being relaxed with one another, trifling, jesting, extending good will and a generous heart to one another. Ailred also mentions activities that build friendship, such as conversing and reading together, thus building common interest, vision and direction.

By touching on the importance of honour, Ailred exhorts us to hold our friends in high regard, respecting one another's different gifts and abilities and seeking to protect one another. Finally, Ailred reminds us that friendship is not about a dull uniformity, but unity and harmony amidst diversity. In this light, friendship is not about conquest, but mutuality. Surely such friendship ought to be celebrated!

We celebrate our friendships by being present and available to one another, sharing common activities as we walk in different ways along a common journey. In the frame of Christian spirituality, we celebrate the common life we share in Christ and the common gift of the Spirit that makes us one in the diversity of our differing personalities and callings.

While friendship involves both the art of affirmation and the gentle art of challenge, it never involves the heavy hand of control. St. Benedict's challenge is therefore appropriate: "The only person who has rights over the inner life of another person is God himself."[3] While the friend challenges, the friend is also longsuffering in the art of the generosity of the heart.

Reflection

Thomas à Kempis reminds us:
"Be more willing to correct yourself
than your dearest friends."[4]

5.2 *Celebrating the Eucharist*

Christ did not give us a creed to live by as much as a feast out of which we live. While creeds can bind people together, they often divide us. And while creeds can give us intellectual certainties, they can also leave with us without heart engagement. Surely the Christian life is about orthodoxy, but orthopraxy is important as well.

To live out of a feast brings some very different melodies into the Christian story. A feast is a communal experience, where we gather together as sisters and brothers in the faith, as friends on a common journey, as pilgrims on the way, as families in solidarity and as seekers looking for one's true home. The joy of feasting with others expands our hearts and pulls us out of our narrow self-preoccupations and social isolation, locating us in the larger picture of community and the slipstream of God's redemptive and healing purposes for humanity. A feast is also about invitation and provision: we are invited to come and partake in the food and drink set upon the table, that we might be sustained for our on-going life journeys.

Within the Christian tradition, this feasting is the eucharistic celebration, where we join in the invitation to partake of Christ made present by Word and Spirit in the symbols of bread and wine, and thus are made more fully one with him. Welcomed, gathered, and nourished by bread and wine, community and the presence of the ever-brooding Spirit, we are encouraged as pilgrims in the faith to journey on in God's calling for our lives. William of St. Thierry makes this clear: "For to eat the Body of Christ [in the Eucharist] is nothing other than to be made the body of Christ and the temple of the Holy Spirit."[5] The Lord's Supper thus shapes us into Christ conformity and community. This means that, like Christ, we live a life of suffering and experience God's resurrection power.

Theophilus of Alexandria points to the healing power of the Eucharist. He writes: "Eat the bread that purges away the old bitterness, and drink the wine which eases the pain of the wound."[6] This feast thus has renewing power, cleansing us from sin and making us whole.

St. John Chrysostom emphasizes the prophetic dimension of the Eucharist: "There is no difference at all between the priest and the layperson, as for example when we are to partake of the awesome mysteries, for we are all alike counted worthy of the same things."[7] This feast makes it impossible for us to leave the table with our social and racial distinctions intact. For this celebration not only reminds us that we belong to Christ; it not only fuels us for the journey of faith; it not only renews us physically and spiritually; but it also calls us to become the new humanity in Christ. As Paul puts it so clearly, "There is no longer Jew or Greek, there is no longer slave or free, there is no longer male or female, for all are one in Christ Jesus" (Galatians 3:28). And again: "For in the one Spirit, we were all baptized into one body—Jews or Greeks, slaves or free—and we were all made to drink of one Spirit" (1 Corinthians 12:13). In the celebration of Holy Communion, we heed a radical call to equality in and through Christ.

Reflection

This paschal meal calls us into a paschal spirituality.
St. Anselm reminds us:
"By virtue of this sacrament I may deserve to be planted into the likeness of your death and resurrection."[8]

5.3 *Celebrating God's Goodness*

Many people find it difficult to declare, let alone celebrate, God's goodness. For some see God as an absent, difficult, controlling perpetrator of violence. If we only look at some of the pages of the Old Testament, with its bloodshed and mayhem, and if we only look at the church in history, this is a fair assessment of God.

But I have become enamoured with the person of Jesus, and as a result I see God through the footsteps of this crucified and resurrected messiah. In Christ, I can celebrate the goodness of God—not simply confessing God as creator and redeemer, but celebrating God's goodness. One of the early Desert Fathers asks, "Tell me, beloved, if thy cloak were torn wouldst [thou] throw it away?" He responds: "Nay, but I would patch it." Then he draws this conclusion: "If thou wouldst spare thy garment, shall not God have mercy on his own image?"[9] Experientially, we know God's goodness when we open ourselves to his grace and embrace, his mending and transforming power. In this, we have much to celebrate.

Julian of Norwich reminds us that God "is quick to receive us" when we come in faith and when we express our needs and failures, "for we are his [God's] delight and joy, and he our salvation and our life."[10] In this relational dynamic, we are blessed and God is glad.

CELEBRATING: A LIFE OF GRATITUDE

But God seeks to get up close and personal. It is one thing to confess in a general way that God sustains my life, but it is quite another to celebrate God's presence, to know God's love and to experience God's renewing power in our lives. The unknown author of *The Cloud of Unknowing and The Book of Privy Counseling* talks about God in deeply personal terms: "Take the good gracious God just as he is, as plain as a common poultice, and lay him to your sick self, just as you are."[11] In this intimate picture, God is like an ointment that brings healing. By way of extension, we can say that God is like a lover who befriends us; God is like a mother who nurtures us; God is like bread that feeds us; God is like a light that lightens our pathway; God is like a guide who shows the way ahead. Thus when we celebrate the goodness of God, we celebrate the God who has drawn close in Christ through the Spirit. We celebrate presence, not concepts.

Yet although we celebrate the goodness of God and all that that means for us in our personal growth and well-being, that is only half the story. As the goodness of God reshapes us, we are called to extend that healing presence to others. St. Clement, Bishop of Rome (c.96), writes: "Take care, my friends, that his [God's] many blessings do not turn out to be our condemnation, which will be the case if we fail to live worthily of him…and do what is good and pleasing."[12] And Paul says: "Blessed be the God and Father of our Lord

Jesus Christ, the Father of mercies and the God of all consolation, who consoles us in all our affliction, so that we may be able to console those who are in any affliction with the consolation with which we ourselves are consoled by God" (2 Corinthians 1:3–4).

Reflection

Julian of Norwich writes,
"For of all the things our minds can think about God,
it is thinking upon his goodness that
pleases him the most."[13]

CELEBRATING: A LIFE OF GRATITUDE

5.4 *Celebration Amidst Difficulty*

No one lives a charmed life. We all have our challenges and difficulties. Despite our status and resources, we are all broken people, and we live in a world that is less than ideal, safe and whole. Our social landscape is marred.

Christians and persons of other faiths have no special status in life that protects them from their own folly and from the precarious nature of our world. We all suffer loss, are sinned against, make mistakes, experience difficulty and have to wrestle with the fact that we are less than what we could be.

St. Anselm speaks of the vulnerable nature of our pilgrim status when he writes, "I weep over the hardship of exile."[14] Our exilic status is two-fold: we are wholly immersed in the ordinary realities of life, while we are seeking to be wholly different in our values and life-style. The unknown author of the *Epistle of Diognetus* (c. 150–225) writes: "They [Christians] share their food, but not their wives. They are in the flesh, but do not live according to the flesh. They live on earth but their citizenship is in heaven."[15]

As we live the ordinary realities of our life *differently*, we can create much space for celebration amidst difficulty and hardship. We don't let circumstances determine our way of life, but rejoice amidst life's contradictions. For in the light of God's good presence with us, we can make sense of what is happening to us—even amidst our sorrows. Speaking of God, the Desert Father Abbot Apollo writes, you "make sore and bindeth up…woundeth and His hands make whole…bringeth low and lifteth up."[16]

Though difficulties may make us defensive, self-pitying and full of blame, they can also shape us to become more self-reflective. Thomas à Kempis writes, "Sometimes it is to our advantage to endure misfortunes and adversities for they make us enter into our inner selves and acknowledge that we are in a place of exile."[17] As we go inward, we may need to confront our fears and insecurities—but we may also discover veins of hope and trust.

Meister Eckhart also speaks of the opportunity for self-evaluation amidst life's misfortunes: "A man [woman] who has been well-off for many years [and] loses it all. He ought then to reflect wisely and thank God for his misfortune and loss, for only then will he realize how well off he was before."[18]

This ancient wisdom suggests that difficulties can create a blessed space that the normal flow of our lives can't provide. At the edges of this unfamiliar boundary, where we may be denuded and de-centered, we may hear and see things that can aid us in our growth and in the mysterious purposes of God.

In this liminal place, we do not discover immediate answers, but must learn to wait. St. Anselm's prayer can become ours: "My consoler for whom I wait, when will you come?"[19] This liminal space may also teach us the art of detachment, as Meister Eckhart writes: "Disinterest [detachment] is best of all, for by it the soul is unified, knowledge is made pure, the heart is kindled, the spirit awakened, the desires quickened, the virtues enhanced."[20]

Reflection

St. Augustine:
"Is not the life of man [woman] on earth an ordeal?
My evil sorrows contend with my good joys."[21]

5.5 *Celebrating Mystery*

The twentieth century, with its major wars, sought rationalistic solutions to shape a new world. At this point in the twenty-first century, we have become somewhat critical about the way in which rationalism has been the dominant way of knowing, and we are open to more relational and intuitive ways of knowing—which opens us to the realm of mystery.

The search for meaning, the longing for God, the practices of spirituality will lead us to walk along the seeking road, where the road's contours and its final destination are wrapped in shrouds of mystery. Instead of being anxious, we should celebrate this mystery, for it is a far more exhilarating experience than plodding along familiar paths of ironclad certainty.

We enter mystery when we wonder about the nature of God. Can we know God only by what God does, or can we enter into the mystery of God's being? How can God be sustaining and transforming the world, while remaining inactive amidst our crises and difficulties? Amidst our own life journeys, why have things turned out differently than we planned or expected? And in our social and cultural world, why are there times of both renewal and revitalization and also institutionalization and decay? Mystery is all around and within us.

CELEBRATING: A LIFE OF GRATITUDE

As we seek to live in tune with the creative Spirit of God, we are invited to live in the expectation of surprise—more open, reflective, consultive, prayerful, and attentive. Embracing this mystery will make us less sure of ourselves, less opinionated and arrogant, less controlling and slower in coming to conclusions.

To begin this precarious journey, we will need to live with humility, as John Cassian reminds us: "If you wish to achieve true knowledge of Scripture you must hurry to achieve an unshakeable humility."[22] And by way of extension, we may say that we need this humility to know ourselves and others and to know God and God's ways. Marguerite Porete reminds us: "Lord, how much do I comprehend of your power, of your wisdom, and of your goodness? As much as I comprehend of my weakness, of my foolishness, and of my wickedness."[23]

Humility is not well thought of in our contemporary world, in part because we have confused it with humiliation and denigration. Yet humility is an awareness of who we are in relation to God and others. We recognize our creatureliness and worship God in love and power. We see and appreciate the goodness of others, recognising our own gifts and limitations.

The arrogant person places himself or herself above others. The person with identity issues and an inferiority complex places herself or himself below others. But persons of humility place themselves in relation to others with respect and appreciation.

In the frame of Benedictine spirituality, humility places us in relation to those who are at the margins of society, for God is present among the lowly, and in the face of the stranger, we may be meeting Christ. But this spirituality also stresses that we place ourselves open to the wisdom of the Abbot and other members of the community.

Reflection

Let us celebrate that humility does not set boundaries, but opens wide spaces.

6

PRAYING:

Nourishing the Inner Life

Prayer is at the centre of our spirituality. In fact, prayer is the very heartbeat of our lives, pulsing as we cry out for help and as we shout in amazement. Our cries of anguish and our exclamations of joy acknowledge that life is bigger than we are and more than we can make of it. In this, we express both our vulnerability and our undeserved happiness. While these responses may not have God in view for everyone, they are forms of prayer nevertheless, for when we call out, we direct that cry to someone—and usually not just the people near or around us.

Prayer, first and foremost, belongs not so much to our religiosity, but to our creatureliness, for it is an expression of our vulnerability, wonder and awe. Thus prayer must not be regarded simply as a pious activity for those in church or the monastery, but as an integral part of our daily lives. Prayer is like breathing, thus prayer techniques are often related to breathing: one breathes out one's anxiety and breathes in God's peace and the gift of the Spirit.

IN THE FOOTSTEPS

It is equally important to realize that prayer is not simply about confession of sin or need, but also exultation, worship and rejoicing. Prayer covers us in times of sorrow as well as joy. Thus we see that the whole gamut of life is the subject of prayer: our cries for mercy, our feelings of gratitude, our calls for help, our expressions of worship, our lament in times of hardship, our impulses to create, our energy to act justly, and our impulses to bow before mystery and all that is holy.

This challenges us to recover the purpose and art of prayer, as many in the Western world see prayer as an irrelevant hangover of the religiosity of the ancient world, a negation of human responsibility, an infantile behavior. Thus we think it is better to act than to pray.

But prayer is never a substitute for action. Prayer does not negate human responsibility, but helps us situate ourselves in sustainable ways in our world. Prayer helps us to see that we are not the grand messiahs of this world. Prayer allows us to acknowledge our human limitations and failures. Prayer empowers us to action and helps us to express our hopes and dreams.

In this way, prayer is a psychological aid that helps us to realize our human limitations as well as our potential. Prayer has a horizontal sweep, taking in all of life, but it also has a vertical dimension. Prayer is an act of transcendence that looks beyond our present realities to what God is doing in our world as we seek to enter the mysterious workings of the Holy Spirit. When we pray, we are longing to befriend God through the revelation of God's personhood in Christ, the mystery of God's being and the strangeness of God's ways with us.

The Christian tradition has mapped out many forms of prayer: prayers of silence, meditation, centering, liturgy, confession, protest and contemplation, to name a few. We are invited to enter into these practices of prayer—not just think about them! Our call is not to pray and then work, but to pray in our work and to work at our prayer.

6.1 *Embodied Prayer*

Many people consider prayer to be an escapist activity, asserting that prayer is a sign of weakness, a crutch that keeps us from fighting our own battles. But prayer is an anticipation and articulation of what one seeks to be and what one knows one must do. In this way, prayer hoists one's flag to the mast, proclaiming not, "I can do this on my own," but rather, "With God's help, this is what I know I must be and do."

When we pray this way, we are not saying, "Lord, do something about this issue or problem." Instead, we are saying, "Lord, make me into what I need to be so that I may respond appropriately to this situation." In other words, we become our prayers. Or, said differently, we embody our prayers.

St. Catherine of Siena writes, "A good man [woman] *is* a prayer."[1] Thus we cannot pray for peace in our world if we are people of violence. We cannot ask God to provide for those in need if we are not marked by generosity. We must become, by the grace of God, the very things we pray for—including how we pray for others. Prayer is not about seeking to change a reluctant God, but about changing those areas of our lives that are unredeemed by the grace of Christ as we seek to serve others.

As we seek the well-being of others, we embody our intercessory prayers. This does not mean that we are always to be the direct answer to prayer, for God may bless others through us or apart from us. But we can be the channels that God may wish to use to heal a broken world.

Polycarp (c. 69–c.155), the bishop of Smyrna in Asia Minor and later a martyr for his faith, exhorts others to pray in this embodied way: "Pray for all the saints. Pray also for kings and magistrates and rulers, and for those who persecute and hate you, and for the enemies of the cross, so that your fruit may be evident among all people."[2] But he himself also embodied this prayer—not only by praying this way while he lived, but even as he died, forgiving those who were about to kill him.

To pray for peace in our relationships and world is one thing, but to become a person who radiates peace and does not retaliate is a living prayer. By embodying our prayers, we draw the future hope of peace into the present. We can also become an embodied prayer by taking the burdens and issues of others into our hearts or upon our shoulders, standing in their place when they do not have the strength or courage to carry on. This is a nutritive form of power, power *for* and *on behalf* of others when they are fearful or weak.

St. Catherine of Siena used to say to burdened and fearful sinners: "Have no fear, I will take the burden of your sins."[3] While this sounds messianic, she was not claiming to forgive sins, but offering to take on the burdens of others: their fears, lack of faith, self-condemnation and even despair.

There are times when we are very vulnerable in our faith journeys—when we cannot give, but need to receive; when we cannot walk, but need to be carried; when we cannot pray, but need to be held in prayer. This is both the joy and the burden of living as the communion of saints. When we are weak, we need others to become embodied prayers for us.

Reflection

Being there for others is a form of prayer.

6.2 *Struggling Prayer*

There is little doubt that most of us struggle with our prayer lives. We neglect prayer when life is "too busy." We find it difficult to pray because we doubt its effectiveness. We are not altogether sure that God even hears our prayers—let alone that God will act through them. Thus the greatest crisis in prayer is a crisis of our relationship with God.

Yet our struggles in prayer are not only in relation to God, but also with ourselves. We see this struggle in St. Augustine's prayer: "Grant me chastity and continence, but not yet."[4] This is an ambivalent prayer of someone who knows where he should be in the call of God and the promptings of the Spirit, yet he is not ready to go there. Thus his prayer reflects inner struggle and turmoil.

In Genesis, Jacob wrestles with a man whom he believes to be Yahweh, and amidst the struggle, he cries out: "I will not let you go unless you bless me" (Genesis 32:26). In this story, Jacob wrestles with God to receive a blessing, which he knows he needs for the next phase in his life's journey.

Here we see Jacob's prayer as a struggle with God for his own sustenance, yet we can also wrestle with God on behalf of others. Abraham pleads with Yahweh not to destroy the people of Sodom in his prayer: "Will you indeed sweep away the righteous with the wicked?" (Genesis 18:23). Then he "negotiates" with God as to the number of righteous that would spare the whole city.

When Yahweh burns with anger because of the people's idolatry in worshipping the golden calf, Moses reminds God that destroying the people he has liberated from Egyptian bondage will throw dishonor on the name of God. He pleads with God: "Turn from your fierce wrath; change your mind and do not bring disaster on your people" (Exodus 32:12). And Yahweh listens to the cry of Moses.

In the Psalms, we hear many cries of struggle: why have you forsaken us? Why do the wicked prosper and your faithful people remain in want? In the book of Job, we hear the cry of a righteous man who does not understand why God has dealt with him in such a harsh way. In the book of Nehemiah, we hear the cry of a man who cannot bear that Jerusalem, the city of shalom, still lies in ruins. And in Jeremiah, we have the voice of a prophet lamenting God's judgment on his people. In the New Testament, Jesus struggles with the will of God in the garden of Gethsemane. Paul struggles with the longing for Christ to be more fully formed in the people within the faith communities that he has established.

We need to recover these prayers of struggle in our time, for we have become far too skeptical about God and God's action in our world, and we stand condemned in our own passivity. We must move from our sullen resignation into active wrestling with God—not the struggle *of* prayer, but prayer that struggles *with* God: prayer that will not let go until God blesses. This form of prayer will change us and our world, for it acknowledges our need of God.

Reflection

Thomas à Kempis describes how Jesus
responds to the cry of our hearts:
"I [Jesus] have come because you have invited me.
Your fears and the yearnings of your soul,
together with your humility and contrite heart,
have moved Me and brought Me to you."[5]

6.3 The Hidden Life of Prayer

Ours is the great age of verbal externalization, as we constantly "put ourselves out there" regarding the activities of our day—no matter how trite and trivial. We want the rest of the world to know what we are doing, almost as if that will prove that we are still here. This feeble cry for significance conveys that our value and importance can only be known when others hear and respond to us.

But beyond the voice of friends and fellow bloggers, there is an inner-knowing that comes from reflective and meditative processes, a knowing comes from a lonely place, where we dare to journey without fear. In this place of stillness, we withdraw in prayer to listen to our hearts and the whispers of the Spirit. In the history of Christian spirituality, this has been called desert spirituality. Wherever we may be in reality, we can enter into this inner stillness, where everything else is stripped away, and we are "naked" before the presence of God, who may well be gracing us with his absent presence.

This inner place of stillness is not active, where we pressure God in order to make things happen. Rather, it is a way of being as we choose to create an empty space where we can lay down our busy social selves, which are always looking for achievement and affirmation. In this empty and lonely place, we can attend to our true "naked" selves, for naked we came into the world and naked we shall leave. Yet the surprise is that in the stupendous love of the God of all grace, this is the place where God will nurture and clothe us with a task. The God who welcomes us into this lonely place is also the God who calls us onto the dusty road.

Though we must withdraw in stillness before the presence of God for our personal well-being, the hidden life of prayer is not only about self-nurture. It is also about friendship with the God, who though wholly fulfilled in the blessed community of Father, Son, and Holy Spirit, is nevertheless marginalized in the world. In this still place, we give God friendship, and we comfort the "lonely" God.

In seeking to comfort God, I ask what God would like me to do. Can I serve you in some particular way? For whom should I pray? Whom shall I visit? In this way, I seek to be the hands and feet of Christ in my own very small and imperfect way as I carry the joy and comfort from my stillness into our rowdy and needy world.

This is very different from frenetic self-actualization. Through prayer, we are still and attentive to the whispers of the Spirit as we seek to do God's will. Though this lonely and restless place may be unfamiliar, boring, scary and frustrating, its "desert" beauty will become a place of delight.

Reflection

St. Jerome (c.342–420) writes about a
pious and noble woman, Paula:
"She was hidden and yet she was not hidden.
By shunning glory she earned glory;
for glory follows virtue as its shadow."[6]

6.4 Different Seasons of Prayer

The spiritual journey is not a smooth pathway, but is marked by uneven territory. Though sometimes we fly along at a great pace, there are long periods of hanging in, along with rough patches of road that bump us off course. Though there may be times of ecstasy, there is also the dark night of the soul and the spirit, as St. John of the Cross describes it.

In our prayer life, there are times of sheer joy, but more often, we pray the long road of perseverance. And though sometimes we hold on through barren times, there are also periods of unfaithfulness and neglect. There are also the changing seasons of life: in youth, our prayers are oriented towards action; but in the latter years of life, our prayers are more reflective. One of the early fathers of Monasticism, John Cassian, understood these different seasons of prayer: "One prays another way when the life of the Spirit is flourishing, and another way when pushed down by the mass of temptation."[7]

For prayer to be a lived reality, we need to recognize its ever-changing form in the kaleidoscope of life. Though we might be stirred to pray in the safety of the sanctuary and the comfort of a small group, we also need to pray amidst the challenges of our jobs, the loneliness of illness, and the long road in the work for justice. Thus prayer is never dull nor uniform, but living and dynamic. This is not to say that liturgical prayers are inappropriate! Rather, a sustaining life of prayer will draw on liturgy to "carry" us through the long prayer tradition of the church, along with our own more spontaneous and personal prayers.

Liturgical prayers remind us of the deeper resources of our faith, and they link us to the wider communion of faith. When we use the Franciscan lectionary *Celebrating Common Prayer* or the Northumbrian lectionary *Celtic Daily Prayer,* among others, we join thousands of others across the globe who are praying these prayers at the same time.

Amidst life's changing realities, Cassian encourages us to anticipate shifting seasons of prayer. In times of revival, our prayers might be confessional and intercessory. In times of transition, our prayers might appeal to God's sustaining presence and wisdom. In times of illness, we might pray for God's faithful and healing presence. And in times of grief, we pray for the courage to let go and accept death.

In difficult times, our prayers may question how God is dealing with us as we seek to understand God's mysterious ways. In the flower of friendship and community, our prayers may be filled with gratitude for rich relationships. And in the long quest for justice in our broken world, we may cry out to God to save us from bitterness, cynicism and anger about the lack of change we see in the world.

PRAYING: NOURISHING THE INNER LIFE

Our prayers need to reflect both woe and joy as we seek to express the realities of life along with the hopes we carry.

Reflection

The unknown author of the *Theologia Germanica* suggests that we need two eyes: "a right eye and a left eye."[8] The right eye is the heavenly glance; the left sees the reality and pain of the world.

6.5 *Cry of the Heart*

When we pray, we are graced by the peaceful presence of God. Sometimes, as we pray, we rest in the joy of our friendship with God, and we rejoice in all that is good. Yet we also cry out to God in doubt and grief, pleading for mercy and hope. There is nothing sophisticated, poetic or liturgical about these prayers, but they express the cries of our hearts. Such prayers acknowledge our need amidst desperate and difficult circumstances. St. John Climacus (c.525–606), Abbot of Sinai and ascetic, writes: "A single word of the publican touched the mercy of God. A single word of faith saved the good thief."[9]

Seeing our own needs or the needs of others may not be as easy as it sounds. Not only do we lack self-knowledge and self-insight, but we are often blind to our greatest needs and faults. Thus there is no cry from our hearts for mercy. We are often far more complacent than we care to admit. And to take this one step further, we do not tend to live with a great sense of the holiness of God and our need for confession and repentance. Somehow we think that we are doing okay, but need God's help from time to time. In living this way, the cry of our hearts is never uttered. We have blanketed ourselves in self-goodwill.

Of course, not all Christians live this way. There are some whose lives are characterized by the struggle for survival, who bear the daily burden of injustice or social exclusion. There are those whose lives are turned upside down by war or natural calamities. They know these desperate prayers for help and justice. And there are others whose lives have been broken by abuse, illness, or disability, or whose lives have been wounded by rejection or neglect. They, too, may know the heart's cry, which can shelter them from bitterness or resignation.

What all of this suggests is that to know one's needs and to bring those needs to prayer is a healthy way to live. To be blind to one's needs and not to bring those needs to prayer is a form of bondage that we deepen through our inability to entrust ourselves to God.

But prayer as the heart's cry is never only about ourselves. We are also invited to cry out to God on behalf of others. This is intercessory prayer, but such prayer can only come through radical identification. The casual bystander or observer does not pray this way, for this form of prayer takes the needs and issues of others onto our own shoulders and into our own hearts. This way of being, living and praying dynamites our self-preoccupation and self-focus. Thus in this form of the heart's cry, we are radically turned around and changed.

Our heart's cry, both in terms of our needs and the needs of others, is a transformative act, in which we are saved both from being blind to our needs and also from hardening our heart, which only leads to other forms of dysfunctionality.

When we cry out for others, we are drawn beyond ourselves into the world's cry for wholeness, peace and justice.

The heart's cry, as Johannes Tauler (c1300–1361), the disciple of Meister Eckhart, has so clearly pointed out is "an ascent of the mind to God," which is "the essence of prayer."[10] Thus our heart's cry does not take place in a vacuum, but reaches out towards God, asking God to stoop down into our lives and circumstances and the needs of others.

This does not mean that we are pulling God out of the heavens, for God may well be ahead of us already. In fact, the sign of God's presence is that we cry out for mercy or help.

Reflection

In this cry we know our true humanity
and acknowledge who God is.

7

PURIFYING:

Embracing the Gift of Purgation

Our forebears saw God as awesome and wonderful. Yet in our contemporary world, we tend to see God more as a convenience, there to help us when we are in some sort of difficulty. Our forebears also saw God as embedded in all of life. Everything was sacred, because all things reflected the presence of God. We tend to see God as far removed from our daily existence. Rather than perceiving God's grandeur in the world, we tend to see the natural world as something to be conquered. Thus our lives are marked by pragmatism rather than a deep spirituality.

Our forebears also had a profound sense of the holiness and purity of God. They saw themselves in the light of these characteristics of God, thus cast themselves on God's mercy as they sought to live in ways that reflected God's light and purity. Theirs was a quest to become like God.

As a consequence, the language of purification and purgation was part of their spirituality. And while that was sometimes expressed in overly ascetic and unhealthy ways, they rightly understood that spiritual growth in becoming more godly involved processes of transformation through cleansing, healing and the practices of asceticism.

In contemporary Christian spirituality, there is an emphasis on transformation as the way to greater fullness of life and wholeness. There is also an interest in healing as a way to personal growth and well-being. Yet we do not often give much thought to how this transformation might occur.

Our ancient forebears teach us that one way to grow towards this wholeness is through purgative processes and the practices of relinquishment and asceticism. In this way, growth does not occur through addition, but rather through being stripped bare.

This invites us to think about spiritual practices that are not so much a part of our contemporary religious landscape, such as: moving towards emptiness rather than fullness, fasting rather than only feasting, voluntary relinquishment rather than much-having, confession rather than rationalization, humility rather than self-enhancement, embracing weakness rather than manipulation, and purgation rather than self-protection.

This very different way of life opens us up to the work of the Holy Spirit in renewing us. It invites us into relationships of openness and accountability. It suggests that the Word of God should not only enlighten us, but also challenge us to greater fidelity. It encourages us to yield our lives to God in new ways,

PURIFYING: EMBRACING THE GIFT OF PURGATION

such that God is not there simply to bless us, but to work his purposes in us.

As we relinquish both what is not good and what may be good, but which God calls us to lay aside, we invite God to become more fully alive within us. These purgative acts of grace make us more truly who we are meant to be, stripped bare of our distortions and compulsions. As we let our wills be bent straight by the fullness of God's love, we truly become the channels of God's life to others.

To be stripped bare by God's way with us neither shames nor humiliates us, but renews us and draws us into God's purposes for our lives and our world.

7.1 *Trials*

All human love and relationships go through the eye of the needle of life's problems and difficulties. Such trials can purify love and make it stronger, able to withstand the hardships of life. Thus loving a spouse marked by debilitating illness is a love purged of fair-weather immaturity.

The Christian journey is no different. Every dimension of the spiritual life—worship, prayer, community and service—will go through difficulties and trials. Though we are saved from our sins, we are not saved from trials. And we might be surprised to discover that where we thought we were strong, we often have weaknesses.

Sadly, in some Christian circles, the trials of life and faith are not talked about. If we acknowledge that we are anything but strong and victorious through Christ, it reflects badly on our spiritual walk. Such a spirituality is clearly marooned in fair-weather immaturity.

Thankfully, our Christian forebears thought very differently. St. Jerome writes openly about his own struggles: "I am no experienced mariner who has never lost either ship or cargo. Lately shipwrecked as I have been myself, my warnings to other voyagers spring from my own fears."[1] Here we have a monumental figure in the Christian church talking not simply about difficulties, but about failure. Whatever the trials were,

PURIFYING: EMBRACING THE GIFT OF PURGATION

Jerome acknowledges that he was shipwrecked. Consequently, his ministry of counsel to others does not come from a place of power and privilege, but from brokenness and humility.

And this introduces us to one of the basic purposes for trials in the Christian life. Trials are meant to try us. They weigh us up. They sift us. And they may well expose us. In times of trial, we are often found to be wanting. We thus discover that we are not as strong and well-integrated as we thought we were.

While this can lead us to discouragement, it is also possible that trials lead us to transformation. As John Cassian explained to a fellow monk, "The Lord allowed you to be hurt so that in your old age you may learn to have sympathy for the weaknesses of others...[and] to reach out to the frailty of the young."[2]

The trials that God allows are not meant to destroy us, but to purge and purify us. Thus we are not to complain about our trials. One often hears: why did God allow this to happen to me? What lies behind this question is the expectation that God will look after us in such a way that no bird dropping should ever fall on our head! But thankfully, this is not God's way with us.

As avenues of growth in our lives, trials test our faith and nurture it into maturity. A faith that has not known the wintry blast of doubt cannot be strong. And a life free from failure is not marked by grace, humility and compassion.

In our growth to maturity in the Christian life, we don't need to seek trials, for they will come our way. While we may pray: Lord, save us from the time of trial. In the midst of trials, our prayer should be: Lord, purify me through your strange ways and so transform me in this time of trial.

Reflection

St. Cyprian puts it well: "God wills us
to be sifted and proved,
as He has always proved his people,
and yet in His trials help has never at any time
been wanting."[3]

7.2 Stubbornness

We are often stubborn and willfully resist the good suggestions of others. Much later, when things have not worked out as we had hoped, we might be able to admit that we should have listened to the advice of others.

Our relationship with God is hardly better. Because we no longer see God in terms of God's awesomeness and power, but as a friend and occasional advisor, we are reluctant to being obedient to God. With the concept of obedience out of vogue, we are living a perennial form of stubbornness and resistance in our self-determined lives.

Thus we are not all that different from those criticized by the prophets and disciples in the Bible. The prophet Ezekiel characterizes the house of Israel as having "a hard forehead and a stubborn heart" (Ezekiel 3:7). And much earlier in the Old Testament, God describes his people as "stiff-necked" (Exodus 33:3). In Stephen's challenge to the religious leaders after the death and resurrection of Christ, he exclaims: "You stiff-necked people, uncircumcised in heart and ears, you are forever opposing the Holy Spirit, just as your ancestors used to do" (Acts 7:51). This way of being and living in relation to God calls for painful judgment, as described by the psalmist: "But my people did not listen to my voice; Israel did not submit to me. So I gave them over to their own stubborn hearts, to follow their own counsels" (Psalm 81:11–12).

While being left alone to determine the course of our own lives may sound like freedom, it is a form of bondage. With no transcendent reference point, no ultimate accountability, and no sustaining Spirit to carry us forward, we are condemned to our own self-reference and resources. What a very lonely and foolish way to live!

The opposite of this willful stubbornness is to live with a loving, obedient heart towards God, as described by the psalmist: "I delight to do your will, O my God; your law is within my heart" (Psalm 40:8). We see this obedience in the Messiah when Jesus exclaims, "My food is to do the will of him who sent me and to complete his work" (John 4:34). The challenge for us as the followers of Jesus is "not to be foolish, but to understand what the will of the Lord is" (Ephesians 5:17). And then, of course, we are called to *live* the will of God.

Between our stubbornness and our submission to the will of God lie painful and challenging processes. One usually does not move happily and easily from one state to the other. Purgation and conversion are the bridges from one way of being to another.

Hildegard of Bingen understood this well. While she wants us to be the willing servants of the living God, she calls us "compelled sheep," whom she describes as "those people who are compelled by Me [God] against their will by many tribulations and sorrows to leave their iniquities."[4]

Here is a picture of God's painful and yet gracious work in us. God will purge us and use whatever lies at the disposal of his tough love. As Jeremiah utters on behalf of Yahweh, "I will chastise you in good measure" (Jeremiah 30:11). So also the author of Hebrews reminds us: "The Lord disciplines those whom he loves, and chastises every child he accepts…in order that we may share his holiness" (Hebrews 12:6, 10).

Reflection

The Desert Father, Abbot Apollo, reminds us that God
"makes the sore and bindeth up…
woundeth and His hands make whole…
bringeth low and lifteth up."[5]

7.3 *Temptation*

As our sense about the presence of a loving God has become weaker in the modern world, so have our notions of evil. Because we have such weak recognition that there are evil forces seeking to seduce us, we lay ourselves open to temptation. We hardly believe in a Satan or Devil that is seeking to draw us away from the things of God, thus we follow blindly after false idols.

Yet in the Old Testament, a Satanic figure is acknowledged (1 Chronicles 21:1; Job 1:6; Zechariah 3:1). In the ministry of Jesus, we see him dealing with evil powers (Luke 7:21), and he is tempted by the devil in the desert and throughout his ministry (Luke 4:1–13). Paul reminds believers: "Do not make room for the devil" (Ephesians 4:27). And James reminds the early Christians: "Resist the devil and he will flee from you" (James 4:7). Peter warns: "Like a roaring lion your adversary the devil prowls around, looking for someone to devour" (1 Peter 5:8). In the story of the deception of Ananias and Sapphira, Peter makes it clear that they were seduced by the devil: "Why has Satan filled your heart to lie to the Holy Spirit and to keep back part of the proceeds of the land?" (Acts 5:5). Thus Christians can be tempted by Satan and become derailed in the process.

PURIFYING: EMBRACING THE GIFT OF PURGATION

But while we can be tempted by outside forces, we can also be tempted within our torn and conflicted inner selves. James writes: "But one is tempted by one's own desire, being lured and enticed by it" (James 1:14).

Our ancient forebears understood this latter dimension of temptation, thus demonstrating profound psychological insight—centuries before Freud! The early Church Father, Origen, writes: "Temptations…serve the purpose of showing us who we really are."[6] And Evagrius (346–399), a native of Pontus and an ascetic writer, makes a similar point: "Many passions are hidden in our soul, but escape our attention. It is sudden temptation which reveals them."[7]

These insights reveal that temptation calls us to discernment. Does this temptation say something about me and my values and world? Or does it say something about the enemy of my soul? While we may prefer to shrug it off as the latter, we need to be reminded that a temptation may have nothing to do with the devil, but everything to do with our conflicted selves.

If temptation reveals what I am denying, that temptation is actually a blessing. Since I can be blind to both my strengths and my weaknesses, temptations can operate as a kind of circuit breaker. When temptation makes me aware of what was hidden from my view about myself, it is an invitation to struggle through a purgative process. I not only have to face the temptation before me, but I have to engage it and decide how to respond.

That which lies hidden inside of me and is brought into the open by temptation is usually no superficial matter. Such deep-seated issues invite a myriad of questions. Is this simply a personal weakness? Is it part of my up-bringing? Is it part on my DNA? It is a generational sin or weakness or aberration? These and other questions challenge me to self-reflection and seeking the help of a counselor or spiritual director.

Thus this opens up a longer—and possibly painful—journey, but it is one that moves from death to life.

Reflection

Thomas à Kempis reminds us:
"You cannot win your crown of patience
without some struggle.
If you refuse suffering, you also
refuse the crown."[8]

PURIFYING: EMBRACING THE GIFT OF PURGATION

7.4 *Surprising Transformation*

Tragedies, health issues, and job losses move us out of our comfort zones and land us in unfamiliar places, where we are often challenged towards new ways of thinking and living. These surprising and unexpected seasons of purgation do not condemn us, but invite us to be cleansed, renewed and transformed.

Yet when the Spirit compels us to go to unfamiliar people or places, we are invited to choose to follow the Spirit into painful places so that we can be transformed. As St. Francis writes: "When I was in sin, it seemed too bitter to me to see lepers. And the Lord Himself led me among them and I showed mercy to them. And when I left them, what had seemed bitter to me was turned into sweetness of soul and body."[9]

What initially seems hard—"bitter"—was turned to joy—"sweetness." Or put differently, what seems to be the hard road may turn out to be easy way. In our contemporary culture, we tend to think that joy can only come from happy occasions and that goodness can only come from well-being. We also think that hardship or difficulty should be avoided, as it can only bring us grief. As a consequence, we tend to waste our sorrows and avoid purgation.

Yet what Francis saw as repelling and unattractive turned out to be a source of blessing and transformation. In the place where he least wanted to be—a place he probably hated—he discovered the transformative grace of the Man of Sorrows.

In the very act of stooping down to kiss the leper, Francis discovered the Christ of Calvary, who stooped down to kiss him. This was not a fleeting experience that soon dissipated by more demanding realities, for it changed Francis forever and became formative for his life and for the religious order he brought into being.

In contemporary Western Christianity, we often want to find the easy road, yet we are called to walk the way of discipleship. We want security, yet we are called to live vulnerably with open hands. We want God's blessings, yet we don't want God's purgative, life-giving processes. We want green pastures, yet our real growth may well depend upon our time in the desert. We want to know, yet the journey of faith is veiled in a cloud of unknowing and shrouded by mystery. We want to be in control, but if we follow the breath of the Spirit, we might be blown in directions where we had not planned to go.

God led St. Francis to the lepers, the very place he did not want to go. Here lies the true secret of the spiritual life: saying "yes" to following God's strange way rather than our more sensible way. Thus we become holy fools for God, troubadours for Christ, prophets of the Kingdom, little ones led by the Spirit.

Reflection

We not only need to be purged of our
sin and wrong-doing.
We also need to be purged of our own wisdom.

7.5 *Eucharistic Purgation*

The word to purge basically means to cleanse or purify. From the Latin, *purgare,* it means to lead to purity. It has many related meanings. In law, it means to clear a person of a charge against him or her. In the political arena, it means to clear out a dissident group within a political party or social movement. In medicine, it means to cause an evacuation of the bowels. And in the religious realm, it means the cleansing from sin. Thus one may say that to be purged is to be purified.

While the term to purge occurs in the biblical narrative (Deuteronomy 13:5; Ezekiel 20:38), the word purify, which is the result of purgative processes, is more common. One frequently hears the prayer, "Create in me a pure heart, O God" (Psalm 51:10). Jesus exclaims, "Blessed are the pure in heart" (Matthew 5:8). And Peter reminds us: "Now that you have purified your souls by your obedience to the truth so that you have genuine mutual love, love one another deeply from the heart" (1 Peter 1:22).

To be pure means to be unmixed or unalloyed. In our spiritual lives, this means a rectification not only of our sinful self, but also of our divided self. Since we are full of mixed motives and desires, to be "pure in heart" means to become

PURIFYING: EMBRACING THE GIFT OF PURGATION

single-minded, resolutely seeking to live to the glory of God rather than the enhancement of our self.

When we appropriate in faith what God has done for us in Christ, we begin a process of purification. Paul makes this clear: "For just as by the one man's disobedience the many were made sinners"—through Adam we became alloyed—"so by the one man's obedience the many will be made righteous"—through Christ our sins are forgiven and we are made right with God (Romans 5:19). The author of the book of Hebrews makes this even clearer: Christ "made purification for sins" (Hebrews 1:3).

Theophilus of Alexandria speaks of the purification process of Holy Communion: "Eat the bread which purges away the old bitterness, and drink the wine which eases the pain of the wound."[10] Participation in the Eucharist, the Lord's Supper, is no mere feast of remembrance, no mere mental projection back to the suffering Christ at Golgotha. Rather, it is an invitation to participate in the living presence of Christ, our food and drink, through the Spirit in the faith community. Paul makes this clear: "The cup of blessing which we bless, is it not a sharing in the blood of Christ? The bread which we break, is it not a sharing in the body of Christ?" (1 Corinthians 10:16).

This food and drink not only nourishes us for the journey of faith, it also renews and cleanses us. When we partake of Christ in this meal of faith, we participate in the whole of Christ. We join Christ as the sacrifice for sin. We join Christ as a healing presence. We join Christ in his resurrection power. We join Christ as the ascended and glorified Lord.

Thus in the Lord's Supper, we participate in Christ's work of justification, sanctification and glorification. And in this way, we are in the process of becoming purged, purified and unalloyed to become more like the One who gave his life for us.

Thus the Eucharist is a transformative feast that moves us from where we are to where we are called to be in Christ. It purges away the old and opens the door to the new. It purifies us so that we can live more fully into the love of God in Christ Jesus. St. Anselm puts this well: "Jesus Christ, my dear and gracious Lord, you have shown a love greater than that of any man and which no one can equal, for you in no way deserved to die, yet you laid down your dear life for those who served you and sinned against you."[11]

Reflection

God not only gives to us. God also takes away.
God not only consolidates. God also transforms.

8

CONTEMPLATING:

Seeing All Things with New Eyes

During the latter part of the twentieth century, people began to question the dominant rational mode of knowing and to speak about the power of intuition and reflection. Within this frame, we have seen a growing interest in the role of contemplation in becoming persons of insight and wisdom. At the same time, those with a religious orientation have begun to use contemplative practices as a way of deepening the life of prayer.

There is no single and simple way to describe the practice of contemplation, but most basically, it has to do with a certain attentiveness. It looks at persons and things to discover a deeper meaning. It is an attempt through reflective processes to get to see the "inside" of things.

Within the religious tradition this means to see God and God's ways more clearly—not only to see who God is in his being, but also to see God's presence and action in the world. And seeing this, we may then understand more fully who we are meant to be and how we are to act in the world.

IN THE FOOTSTEPS

The most basic movement in contemplation is the move away from in order to be with, so that we might see, hear and be empowered to re-engage our circumstances and world with newfound insight and energy. The move away from is the practice of withdrawal, stillness and receiving the gift of solitude as we leave behind our busy routines and world. One could call that the move into the "desert," the solitary place, wherever that may be in one's house, office or in creation.

But one does not move away from one's normal routines simply for its own sake. One moves away in order to make space to be with the One we so readily and easily neglect in the daily realities of our lives. The move to be with is shaped by the practices of prayer, meditation and receiving the gift of contemplation. This is a movement of transcendence.

In the move to the "desert," we become still, denuded, naked and vulnerable in order to prepare the way to encounter and be with God. This being with God is not first of all to gain something, for this would only be a form of manipulation or pragmatism. Rather, this way of being with God is about relating with God, being loved and nurtured by God. It has to do with being attentive and listening. It is not focused on our own needs, but with what God wants and what God gives.

Clearly, when we come to be with God in our "nakedness" and in humility of heart, we are not a blank slate. We bring our whole selves, which includes the issues of our lives and the situations of our world. But we come to be with God, to lay all before God, and to hear what God might say to us. For God created us, and when we are with God in prayer, God will always call us to a task.

When we are with God in this relational and reflective way, we are to take what God gives us back into our world, and this is the movement of immanence. Sometimes God gives a nurturing silence. Sometimes God gives the gift of love. And sometimes God gives insight into who we are to become and what we are to do. Thus we are to be contemplatives in both prayer and action. In our service, we are to be prayerful; and in our prayers, we are to serve the world.

As a consequence, contemplatives are not those who hold to a world-denying form of Christianity. Rather, they hold to a world-formative Christianity. Their spirituality is not escapist, but oriented towards costly service. Thus it could well be that contemplatives are the real radicals in our world.

8.1 *The Vision of God*

The heart of Christian spirituality has little to do with having special ecstatic experiences. While some may long for such encounters, particularly in our celebrity culture where one can publicly boast about such things, the heart of Christian spirituality lies with the vision of God.

The vision of God sought by Moses, but most clearly apprehended by Christ, is about God and the worship of God. This vision does not give special status to the seeker; rather, it is about our need for grace, forgiveness and healing so that we might gain a servant heart.

In contemplation, we seek to see God beyond our stereotypes and hang-ups, beyond anything we can gain. We seek to see God and worship God for who God is alone.

Meister Eckhart understood this well. He writes that we are "to seek nothing and to set out only for God himself." When we do this, we "discover God who gives the seeker all that is in his divine heart."[1] Thus in this encounter we receive what God chooses to give, not what we hope to gain. And what God decides to impart, while it is always cast in grace, may be the joy of the Spirit or the call to suffer. It may be that God wishes to give abundance, but God may also seek to strip us bare.

CONTEMPLATING: SEEING ALL THINGS WITH NEW EYES

While this may sound scary for some, as it suggests that we are not in control, when we move towards God in this vulnerable way, we learn to trust God's otherness and lordship, and so we welcome God's strange ways with us. For we believe that all of God's ways—the blessed and the difficult—will lead us along the path of righteousness. On this path, God will never abandon us nor leave us to walk alone. Though we may stumble, we trust God to guide and lead us with his rod and staff (Psalm 23).

This way of relating to God will call us to make huge changes, for we don't naturally relate to God in this way. We want God to be there for us, not the other way round! Yet the unknown author of *The Cloud of Unknowing* encourages us to be more present to God than to ourselves: "Attend more to the wholly Otherness of God rather than your own misery."[2] This is not what we want to hear. This is not the God *for us* that we have sculpted in our own imagination. The God we want is the God who is there to help us.

When we gain the vision of God that is all about God and not simply about us, we receive a great gift. Only the Spirit can sculpt such a vision at the very core of our being. Bonaventure understands this well when he writes: "The reader might think that reading is sufficient without heavenly anointing, or thinking without devotion, or investigation without admiration, or mere observation without rejoicing, or effort without piety, or knowledge without charity, [or] endeavour without divine grace."[3]

This Franciscan theologian suggests that thinking and piety belong together and that our efforts need to be superseded by the impulses of the Holy Spirit. Thus to gain the vision of God or the passion for union with God, which lies at the heart of the ancient Christian wisdom, is never a human achievement. It is a gift that comes through God's generous gratuity.

All our spiritual practices, including our acts of costly service, are not the means to bring us closer to God in order to capture the vision of God. Rather, the vision of God is God choosing to draw near to us. Out of this, our spiritual practices and acts of service find their inspiration.

Reflection

In my journey towards you, O God,
I am carried by your life-giving Spirit.

8.2 *The Practice of Solitude*

At the very core of our humanity, we are sculpted by restlessness and conflict. As we seek inner cohesion and peace, this restlessness may compel us to incessant activism, as if we can justify our existence through what we do and achieve. Yet this is not a good way to find inner peace, for we readily say to ourselves that we have not done enough—and so seek to do more and more, further depleting our inner resources.

A more productive journey toward inner peace is to reflect on the nature of our inner restlessness and conflict. And here the biblical story of our loss of innocence and our loss of God's unmediated presence become startlingly relevant. The truth is that we have lost our true home, and we are in flight mode. The challenge for us is to find our way home again.

But again, the biblical story is wonderfully clear, as it reveals how God sought us out and provided the way for our homecoming. In Christ, God made a way for our complete healing and restoration.

In this homecoming to God and ourselves, we are invited to engage in the spiritual practice of solitude. The practice of solitude helps us to face our inner restlessness and to confront the compulsive behaviours that flow out of that restlessness. When we engage the practice of solitude, we recognize that God has already provided a resting place for us, and we do not need to deplete ourselves in a futile search that we will never fulfill on our own. In solitude, we enter the home of our salvation through Christ, and we embrace the God who created that home for us.

One dimension of the practice of solitude is to find a place of stillness. Jacques de Vitry, the thirteenth-century cleric who wrote *The Life of Mary of Oignies* about a Medieval mystic, notes: "Silence and stillness please our Lord so much."[4] And Thomas à Kempis adds: "Set aside an opportune time for deep personal reflection and think often about God's many benefits to you."[5]

A place of stillness needs to combine with an inner stillness, and this is the gift we receive when we cease from our own striving. Instead of finding well-being through our own efforts, we are loved in God for who we are in God's grace. This is to enter the true Sabbath that God has prepared for us.

This dynamic gives the Christian practice of solitude a particular flavour. Since solitude literally means to be alone, in Christian spirituality there is another dimension to this basic meaning. Yes, we are alone in this place of stillness. We have separated ourselves from others and from our normal rhythms of life. But we are not alone for the sake of being alone. We are alone in order to be with.

To put this in somewhat different terms, we may say that in the practice of solitude we are horizontally alone in order to be vertically connected. We withdraw in order to connect. And the movement of this connection is to leave aside for a brief time our fellow travelers with whom we are so embedded in order to deepen our relationship with the God we so easily neglect.

And in being alone with the God we so often marginalize, we not only find God, but we also find ourselves. In finding God more fully, we find the true centre of our own existence. And in finding God and ourselves, we are better placed to play our part in the journey of companionship and community with others.

When we know ourselves more fully in the lonely place, the place of stillness and reflection, which is the place of listening and attentiveness, we may well move to worship and prayer. But we may also move to new ways of engagement.

Having been enlightened by the wisdom of God through the Spirit in this place of quiet reflection, we may be guided to enter the fray of life with different motivations and perspectives. Instead of enmeshment, we may find a new freedom in solidarity. Instead of social conformity, we may find a new prophetic boldness.

Reflection

Don't be afraid to be alone. There you may be truly found.

8.3 *The Contemplative Experience*

Some express concern that contemplation can lead us away from God and hearing God's voice through Scripture by becoming inwardly preoccupied with our own inner voices. Some also fear that contemplation can lead us away from concern and involvement with our world by becoming too focused on the world to come.

But the contemplative experience need not and should not be expressed in these ways. In contemplation, we become attentive, reflective and prayerful as we seek to see through something to discover its heart or essence. In this multi-dimensional practice, we relate to God, ourselves and the world. Thus in contemplation, we come see God more clearly, ourselves more truly and the concerns and issues of our world more insightfully.

This experience can draw us into a fuller relationship with God. Jan van Ruysbroeck makes this clear: "All our powers then fail us and we fall down in open contemplation. All become one and one becomes all in the loving embrace of the threefold unity. When we experience this unity, we become one being, one life, and one blessedness with God."[6]

This is a powerfully transformative experience that has wider implications. For when God becomes our true centre, we begin to see everything else with new eyes. When God is

CONTEMPLATING: SEEING ALL THINGS WITH NEW EYES

seen and experienced as Lord, everything else becomes relativized to that reality, and there can be no other lords. The powers of our culture are no longer perceived as being all that powerful. This vision of God brings us into a freedom to become the prophets of our time.

In the contemplative experience, we are attentive to God in order to see through things, and we are attentive to the Spirit moving and working within us, bringing renewal, inspiration and new vision. As St. Clare (1194–1253), a follower of St. Francis and foundress of the Poor Clares, writes, contemplation is "seeing with the eyes of the Spirit."[7]

But we also need to be attentive to what is going on around us. We need to see through what is happening in our families, our institutions and our world. Thus we are contemplatives on the mountaintop of spiritual enlightenment, and we are contemplatives in the valleys of daily life as we actively engage the issues of our time.

It is important to note that the contemplative experience is revelatory, coming as a gift and surprise. As the unknown author of *The Cloud of Unknowing* writes, "One loving blind desire for God alone is more valuable in itself, more pleasing to God and to the saints, [and] more beneficial to your own growth…than anything else you could do."[8]

Yet if we only pray about our world without engaging it in costly service, our insights will be limited. Insight comes both from withdrawal and engagement. In prayer and in action, on the mountaintop and in the valleys of life, in the faith community and in the world of business, we are called to be contemplatives, moving from reflection and discernment into what we must do to impact our world.

Reflection

St. Anselm encourages us to pray as follows:
"Hear me always with your favour, not according as my mouth wills or my mouth asks,
but as you know and will that I ought to wish and ask."[9]

CONTEMPLATING: SEEING ALL THINGS WITH NEW EYES

8.4 *Christification*

One of the pitfalls of Medieval Christianity is that its emphasis on piety and living the Christian virtues, including generosity through almsgiving, can give the impression that the Christian life requires huge self-effort in becoming more godly. Thus the Reformers of the sixteenth century emphasized our justification by faith in the finished work of Christ on the cross on our behalf. God's work in us through the process of sanctification flowed from justification, but it called forth our cooperation.

Whether the Reformers, and particularly Martin Luther, placed the work of God's salvation in too juridical terms will always be a subject for debate. But the concept of exchange, namely that Christ as the sinless One exchanges his blessings with us as sinful ones, is not the whole story of God's redemptive work in our lives. The completion of the story is that we are called to become more Christlike.

St. Simeon, the New Theologian and Abbot of the Monastery of St. Mammas in Constantinople (949–1022), writes: "The ineffable birth of the Word in the flesh from his mother Mary is one thing, his spiritual birth in us [is] another."[10] Following the Johannine gospel, we place an emphasis on being born again, yet we also need to speak of the "double birth" of Jesus. Jesus is born of Mary, but Jesus also needs to be born in us.

The birth of Jesus through Mary was a work of the hovering and fructifying Spirit. The birth of Jesus in us as members of the body of Christ is also a work of the Spirit. Thus in the Spirit, Jesus makes his home in us, and this is the process of Christification.

Christification is the process of becoming Christlike. This occurs not simply by our attempts to imitate Christ in a life of discipleship, but through an inner shaping and forming of the life of Christ in us through the Spirit.

In Christification, piety and mission come together in an integrated way. Christlike virtues grow in our lives as we serve the world in conformity to Christ. Thus like Christ, we seek to proclaim the good news of the Kingdom and to be a healing presence in the world; we, too, seek to push back the powers of darkness and to challenge the religious status quo; we, too, seek to build an alternative form of community and to care for the poor. Following the path of Christ, we seek fellowship with the Father, and we seek to live and work in the power of the Spirit. And like Christ, we become people of prayer and action.

Thus Christification is not simply the process of shaping an inner piety, but also becoming the suffering and transforming presence of Christ in the world. Through the Spirit, we continue the Christ project, which is that Christ—as the New Adam and head of the new humanity—may take gestalt in all of our lives, reshaping our institutions and our world.

Our hope and prayer therefore is that Christ may be born anew in each of our lives and that this birth may give birth to the new creation that the Spirit of the Living God is seeking to birth and breathe into being.

Reflection

William of St. Thierry invites us to follow this Christ: "Our most powerful athlete having entered as it were the stadium of the world, was anointed with the oil of the Holy Spirit for the match and rejoiced as a first to run the course of [the] human dispensation."[11]

8.5 *Meditating on the Word*

In Christian spirituality, we must be wary of several one-sided emphases. We cannot focus on the Holy Spirit without holy Scripture—the Word of God—as this can lead to a free-wheeling subjectivism where our creative imaginations run wild. We also cannot control the Word without the inspiration of the Holy Spirit, as this can lead to a rigid dogmatism. When we think we have all the answers, a crusader mentality can run riot, because we think that we possess the truth rather than the truth possessing us.

Clearly, Word and Spirit belong together, and we are invited to find ways of engaging Scripture so that the Spirit can enlighten us and the Word can be woven into the fabric of our being. In this way, the Word becomes a living Word through the Spirit, making a home within us, determining our choices and values and shaping our whole life.

While Scripture can be engaged in a scholarly way, it also needs to be engaged in a reflective and prayerful way. The early Christian writing of the first or second century, *The Epistle of Barnabas,* speaks of this latter approach: there are those "who know that meditation is a delight—who do in fact chew the cud of the Lord's Word."[12]

One classical expression of a meditative approach to scripture is *Lectio Divina.* This has a number of important inter-related elements. The first element, *lectio,* involves a slow repetitive reading of a particular portion of scripture. One may read a passage aloud or to oneself three or four times. This, in itself, is an important act, since we are usually in a hurry and claim that we are constantly time poor. The second element, *meditatio,* involves a concentrated reflection on a word, phrase or concept that has stood out to the reader during the *lectio.* In this, one engages Scripture in terms of personal appropriation, and the ancient Word becomes a living word for our life and circumstances. In faith, this is where we hear God speaking to us through a word of encouragement, correction or direction.

When we hear such a word for our life in faith, we are called to the next element, *oratio,* or prayer. We praise God for who God is and thank God for speaking to us. We ask God for discernment and wisdom regarding the things we believe God is saying to us. In this element, we move to *discretio,* where we ask God's light to shine upon us and guide us.

Having heard and prayed and in faith sensing that the Spirit is leading and guiding us, we need the blessing of the next element, *consolatio,* which is the gift of comfort, hope and courage. God is not only guiding us, but will also be with us. We are not alone. The breath of the Spirit will lead us forward. With the gift of consolation, we are then called to the next element, the *deliberatio,* which is the motivation of our will and the making of appropriate commitments. We say, "Yes, Lord, I have heard your voice and I will do what you ask." This is the spirituality of obedience, which leads to the next element, *actio,* which is the outworking of this word of direction in the daily realities of life.

This is one way of understanding the contemplative experience, as it brings together both Word and Spirit, prayer and action. In *Lectio Divina,* we hear the Word of God and let it guide us, transform us and move us to serve our world.

St. Bernard of Clairvaux captures the essence of this well: "The revelation which is made by the Holy Spirit gives light so that we may understand and fire so that we may love."[13] For St. Bernard, enlightenment clearly leads to service. The revelation of God calls us to become godly—and to be godly is to act in God's way in the world.

St. Francis reminds us: "Inwardly cleansed, interiorly enlightened and inflamed by the fire of the Holy Spirit, may we be able to follow in the footsteps of Your beloved Son."[14] Inner transformation leads to discipleship. Contemplation leads to action.

CONTEMPLATING: SEEING ALL THINGS WITH NEW EYES

Reflection

It all begins by an attentive listening to God
through his word and by his Spirit.
We can never fully imagine what the fruit of this may be.
It may well change many things.

9

JOINING:

The Mystery of Community

While it is true that God is interested and concerned about each one of us as individuals, it is also true that God seeks to build a people. There are some profound reasons why Christian spirituality is not simply about the empowerment of a bunch of isolated individuals.

The first and foremost reason why God builds a people is because God is a community of "persons." The God of the biblical narrative and of later theological reflection is the God who is Father, Son and Holy Spirit.

While some of Paul's epistles end with the terse blessing: "May the grace of our Lord Jesus Christ be with your spirit" (Galatians 6:18), others end with a Trinitarian benediction: "The grace of the Lord Jesus Christ, the love of God, and the communion of the Holy Spirit be with you all" (2 Corinthians 13:13).

From these and other passages the vision was born that God is not a monad but a fellowship in unity and mutuality. Father,

JOINING: THE MYSTERY OF COMMUNITY

Son and Holy Spirit live in and for one another in perfect love and harmony.

Becoming a Christian, therefore, is to come home to the love of the Father through the grace of the Son in the power and renewing work of the Holy Spirit. It is to be welcomed into the "family" that God is and to grow in the knowledge of God as creator, redeemer and beautifier. It is to be indwelt by this Trinitarian God, as John makes so startlingly clear with the words of Jesus: "And we will come to them and make our home with them" (John 14:23).

If our lives become, through faith, intertwined with this Trinitarian God, then our orientation will not be towards individualism but towards community. We will be constantly exploring what we have in common with this God and with each other. Or put another way, the common life we have in God through the salvation of Christ and the bonding work of the Spirit will impact the kind of human community we are seeking to build.

Thus what binds Christians together is not only a set of common beliefs or common practices, although these are very important, but a more fundamental common identity. That is to say, community is not first and foremost practical but ontological. Christ gives us a common salvation, and the Spirit binds us all to himself and to each other. Through the waters of baptism and the vivifying work of the Spirit, we are made one in Christ and so become the body of Christ.

This raises the question: what then do we have in common? The early church fathers responded: all things except our wives. And the Didache, a first- or second-century Christian teaching manual makes clear: "Do not turn your back on the needy, but share everything with your brother [sister] and call nothing your own. For if you have what is eternal in common, how much more should you have [in common] what is transient."[1]

Clearly this poses a challenge to us in the modern world. We may be happy to engage in common activities, such as singing common hymns of praise or making a common confession in the Apostles Creed or joining together in common acts of service, but we continue to hold on to our private existence. Yet it should be the other way round! We should be committed to a common life in Christ with a certain amount of privacy.

JOINING: THE MYSTERY OF COMMUNITY

9.1 *The Voice of the Least*

Church communities are, for the most part, run as organizations or sometimes even businesses. This is a challenge for our time, as the church is called to be a community of people who share a common faith and a common life in Christ. Though we accept sharing common beliefs, the sharing of a common life is more controversial, because we have separated word and deed, faith and lifestyle, the spiritual and the practical, the heavenly and the earthly. Thus we are happy to celebrate our common spirituality as Christians, yet we resist being one in a common way of life.

In defense of this dichotomy, we readily cite history: we have monks to live church as a community, and the rest of us to live church in an ordinary way. Yet throughout the history of the church, so-called "ordinary" Christians have sought to live in intentional Christian community. We need only think of the Brethren of the Common Life in the past and the L'Arche communities in the present.

Moreover, the early Christians did not live "ordinary" lives, for in Acts 2 and 4, we see them living a communal form of life. And St. John Chrysostom reminds us: "Those who live in the world, even though married, ought to resemble the monks in everything else."[2] And St. Augustine, the Bishop of Hippo who lived in a community, speaks of Christians forming "common households" which "were to have one purse and the whole was to belong to each and all."[3] This is very challenging to us "ordinary" Christians.

To move towards this vision of commonality, we need to see one another as united in the faith rather than separating one another by gender and status, clergy and laity, or higher and lower spirituality. When we view one another across these divides, this leads to an unhealthy judgmentalism that separates people rather than building community.

One of the Desert Fathers alerts us to this matter: "See that thou despise not the brother that stands by thee: for thou knowest not whether the Spirit of God be in thee or in him."[4] This calls us to live beyond our normal social distinctions. This moves us away from our normal organizational categories and pulls us into commonality and community. This calls us to live in a new humility, for God can use anyone in the community as a bearer of his word or wisdom. And this follows the movement of the incarnation, where God in Christ becomes a human, the suffering servant.

God's strange way of downward mobility is to become our way. Not the way of organizational prestige, but the way of the humiliation of the Word who became flesh. This way is the way of community, a life of service that gives all.

Christian community, whether in church or in intentional community, is not first about certain structures, but about seeing others through the salvation that Christ gives and recognizing that being bound to Christ links me to my brothers and sisters in the faith.

This connection is both spiritual and practical. It is about love and care, availability and service, and a willingness to receive from others—even from "the least."

Reflection

The unknown author of the *Epistle of Diognetus*
describes the early Christians as follows:
"They share their food but not their wives.
They are in the flesh, but do not live according to the flesh.
They live on earth, but their citizenship is in heaven."[5]

9.2 *Seeking the Common Good*

One of the great temptations on the part of those living in intentional Christian community is to see what they have as a possession. They possess a different way of life and a different set of values, and this makes them feel happy and secure, perhaps even prideful that they are living the gospel with greater fidelity.

But community is not a possession. It is first and foremost a gift of grace. Only in and through Christ, by the inspiration of the Holy Spirit, can Christian community come into being.

Not only is Christian community a gift of grace, but it is what we seek to become and grow into. Thus it is not a possession nor an aspiration, but a pathway for us to become more fully who we already are.

The unknown author of the *Letter of Barnabas* opens this up for us: "Do not withdraw within yourselves and live alone, as though you were already justified, but gather together and seek out together the common good."[6] This fascinating instruction suggests that we can't be solo Christians, but are encouraged to gather together. And one way to do that is not only to gather in church for common worship on Sundays, but also to gather together in other ways and at other times. One common form of that in many urban centers is cluster living. In this configuration of intentional community, a group of Christians live within walking distance of one another. They may meet during the week for worship, learning and fellowship. They may share resources such as tools, lawn movers, cars. They may share some meals. And they are united in a common mission in their neighbourhood.

But the writer also speaks of the call to seek the common good, and this is three-directional: upward, inward and outward. The upward movement is to seek together the face of God by entering more fully into a relationship with God. This is the movement of transcendence. Through scripture, worship, prayer and meditation Christians in their life together are called to orient themselves towards God in order to be safe, welcomed, nurtured, empowered and directed by the God who loves them and gives them a task.

The inward movement has to do with building the common life of the community. Though the upward movement enriches the life of the community, the community must also grow in finding practical ways to nurture their life together. And at this point, the community needs to discern whether all are blessed and being encouraged to grow, for some might benefit at the cost of others. This does not mean imposing a grey and dull uniformity, but rather nurturing a rich diversity within a core and committed unity. Though such community is not a possession, it must be maintained, recovered at times and constantly revitalized.

The outward movement draws on God's goodness and seeks to extend that goodness by becoming servants to the world. But a community can only unfold its life together into the world when God's goodness has shaped the life of the community by the power of the Spirit. Thus we seek to be to the world what we already are before God and what we are in relation to one another.

Reflection

Maximus the Confessor reminds us:
"The one who imitates God by giving alms knows no difference between…just and unjust."
The Christian "distributes to all without distinction according to their need."[7]

9.3 *A Radical Freedom*

Some think that various forms of intentional Christian community, whether monastic communities or more contemporary forms of cluster living, are restrictive places of numbing conformity. And many Christians see this way of religious existence as unattractive and outmoded in the modern world. For we have become enamored with the idea that we are self-made persons, thus we constantly have to feed our ever-expanding selves with new experiences, new jobs, and new relationships.

In contrast, we think that community will rob us of these possibilities and stultify us, restricting us to one place and preventing us from becoming the persons we can be. The logic here is that the wider we go, the more we will enhance the self. Yet this does not recognize that the deeper we go may form us more truly into the persons we are meant to be.

Thus to remain deeply and gratefully connected to one's family of origin, to remain in one's marriage, to follow through on one's vocation, to continue to journey with one's friends and to be embedded in a faith community can be deeply life-giving. These commitments are not automatically death-dealing, though when they become destructive, we do have to move on.

But how can being part of an intentional community provide radical freedom rather than dulling conformity? First, this way of living life is a small reflection of the Trinity, for God is a community of persons and God reflects a richness of life in love and mutuality. Thus as the people of God, indwelt by Father, Son and Holy Spirit, we are invited to live life in similar ways.

Secondly, the biblical narrative is clear that God seeks to build a people. In the Old Testament, Israel was called to be light to the nations. In the New Testament, the body of Christ was called to be a community beyond all ethnic, gender and class distinctions and to witness to God's redemptive work in Christ. Thus as a people, we are to reflect who God is, what God has provided and what God is doing in the renewal of all humanity and the world.

Thirdly, living in some form of intentional community, rather than only participating in Sunday worship, helps us to live a life of giving and receiving. It helps us to give legs to the idea that we are not only bound to Christ in faith through the Spirit, but we are also connected in love and service to our brothers and sisters in the faith. Community is thus a sacramental way of living the body of Christ.

Finally, a corporate faith is a fuller witness to the world than a solo faith. In a life together, we can reflect something of the beauty and greatness of who God is.

JOINING: THE MYSTERY OF COMMUNITY

If power is not misused, prayer is not neglected, humility is cultivated, hospitality is practiced, and service to the world is evident, then such a community is a place of freedom, not conformity.

St. Benedict underscores this freedom. He writes: "The only person who has the rights over the inner life of another person is God himself."[8]

Reflection

St. Clement reminds us:
"Take care, my friends, that his [God's] many blessings do not turn out to be our condemnation, which is the case if we fail to live worthily of him… and do what is good and pleasing."[9]

9.4 *Radical Sharing*

The *Epistle of Diognetus* reminds us that as Christians we are to live "the unusual character of our citizenship."[10] This terse statement suggests that the Christian way of life is not simply a personal reality, nor is it simply an inward reality; rather it is a corporate way of life visible to the watching world.

One way in which the Christian way of life is made more visible is through various forms of community. And one of the key characteristics of such a community is radical sharing.

This way of living has its source in the recognition that Christ has made us one and that the love we have for Christ is also to be expressed in practical love and care for each other. St. Ambrose reminds us of this fundamental oneness. He writes: the church "pours the same grace not only upon the rich and mighty, but also upon men [women] of low estate, she weighs them all in an equal balance, gathers them all into the same bosom, cherishes them in the same lap."[11]

If we are one in Christ then this can never be purely a spiritual reality. It also has to become practical, and St. Ambrose suggests that all persons are to be treated in the same way. St. Augustine takes this one step further. He writes: a person's "possession of goodness is in no way diminished by the arrival…of a sharer in it; indeed, goodness is a possession enjoyed more widely by the united affection of partners."[12]

While St. Augustine is not speaking specifically about sharing financial resources, the point he is making includes practical sharing. What he is saying is counter-intuitive, for in our age of much-having and an insatiable longing for security, we think that sharing diminishes us. St. Augustine suggests the opposite: we are not diminished, but rather enriched, by sharing.

In the web of mutual relationships, as we give and receive, all are enriched. The giver is deepened in his or her generosity and learns to live life with a greater sense of openness. The receiver is deepened in gratitude by what she or he receives. This way of life is a striking counter balance to the lust to possess and control that so characterizes contemporary life.

While St. Francis challenges us to live "without personal possessions"[13] in a fraternal community of radical equality, and St. Augustine wants common households in which "all were to have one common purse and the whole was to belong to each and all,"[14] there are many other ways to live radical sharing.

One way is to make oneself available to others in friendship, companioning, advising and mentoring. This sharing of oneself and one's life experience and wisdom is a wonderful way to be there for the other and to benefit and enrich that person.

Another way is to practice hospitality, inviting others—even strangers—into one's home and life. Hospitality may simply be sharing a meal, but it can also be extending a place of safety, refuge and care to another for a period of time.

A further way of radical sharing is in the spiritual practice of prayer. In praying for others and in bringing their burdens and issues into the presence of God, I am sharing my spiritual energies on behalf of others.

And of course, radical sharing involves sharing my financial resources with others. The conversion of the heart is one thing, but the conversion of one's wallet is quite another. This conversion involves breaking the power of Mammon (money) through generosity.

At this point, Meister Eckhart's reminder is appropriate: "do all you can in the way of good works solely for the praise of God…You shall not ask anything in return for it and then your efforts will be both spiritual and divine."[15]

Reflection

What needs to change in me
so that I may live life with open hands?

JOINING: THE MYSTERY OF COMMUNITY

9.5 *Radical Identification*

For most people in the contemporary world, to be with another person in church is no different than seeing that same person in the supermarket, at the ballet or at a football match. Our sense of connection to others in church is tenuous because we tend to regard one another simply as fellow participants in a common activity. Though we "do" church together, our lives are not connected in other significant ways.

This reality stems from a host of practical reasons. In urban settings, churches have a large turnover rate as people move to live elsewhere or choose another church for a multitude of reasons. Moreover, the common worship activities in most churches are not relationally connecting, and passing the peace with a smile and a handshake often remains a mere, though well-meant, formality. Yet the most fundamental reason for this lack of connection is that our faith orientation is primarily vertical and only remotely horizontal. In other words, our central link is with Christ, and our link with one another is peripheral.

Thus we have little practical experience that our confession is "a communion of saints." Put differently, we have only a vague notion of what it means to be the body of Christ. As a consequence, we do not perceive our connection to one another through our common connection with Christ and through the unifying work of the Holy Spirit. Our poor connection as a body reveals how our culture, with its individualism, pragmatism, consumerism and functionalism, has invaded the sanctuary. We are far more culturally captive than we care to acknowledge.

We need to recover in our time the recognition that being baptized into Christ also means being baptized into the body of Christ, the faith community. The double-face of this baptism means that how I relate to members of the church reflects how I relate with Christ; and how I relate with Christ is expressed in how I serve members of the church. If our love for fellow members of the body of Christ is weak, we can only conclude that our love for Christ, despite what we think or say, is also weak.

St. Ignatius reminds us that "those who profess to be Christ's will be recognized by their actions."[16] The early Christian writing the *Didache,* most probably from the second century, spells out what those actions can mean: "Do not turn your back on the needy, but share everything with your brother [sister] and call nothing your own. For if you have what is eternal in common, how much more should you have [in common] what is transient."[17] And Abbot Antony, one the early Desert Fathers, speaks about the dynamic link between us and God and our sisters and brothers in the faith: "If we do good to our brother [sister], we shall do good to God; but if we scandalize our brother, we sin against Christ."[18]

All these quotations point in the same direction, reminding us of the mystery and responsibility of the communion of saints. They reveal that the flip-side of belonging to Christ is to belong to a faith community. Our belonging cannot be merely casual, but involves a life of sharing—and sharing not only our common worship and prayer concerns, but also our time and resources.

The life we have in Christ, through the Spirit, is a life together. Though this can take many forms, fellow members of the body are not casual acquaintances. Our friendship with Christ calls us to outwork that relationship amidst the body.

Reflection

Richard Rolle prayed "that Christ may stable [in] us."[19]

A common Christ amongst us means a common life.

10

SERVING:
The Joy of Self-Giving

In Christian circles, the concept of serving is often linked to voluntary activity that we do in and for the church or in the service that we extend to others outside of the faith community. For some, Christian service is confined primarily to the task of witnessing so that others may come to faith in Christ. For many others, witnessing needs to be augmented by other forms of service, such as care for the needy and the work of seeking justice. But there is so much more to the idea of service, for it is related to everything we do when we don't have only ourselves in view. Service is a form of self-giving as a key expression of our love for others.

We are called to serve God, and we do so in worship. This is a theme in the liturgical tradition of the Christian church. We serve God in prayer, attentiveness and contemplation. But we also serve God when we wash the feet of the world and when we do the work of justice. What we do for the least, we do for Christ himself.

SERVING: THE JOY OF SELF-GIVING

We are called to serve our families, and we do so in relationships of care and solidarity. We serve our families through the whole journey of life, including in the aging of grandparents and parents or the ill-health of siblings. As we walk alongside our family through the long journey of ill-health, the slow slide into dementia or other forms of deterioration, we are deeply challenged to continue to serve and be attentive to them them as fully we as we can.

We are also called to serve the community of faith, both locally and more widely. We are to be in solidarity with and walk as companions alongside our sisters and brothers in the Majority world—as much for their sake as for ours. We are called to serve the church faithfully in dry seasons of the church's life as much as in its times of revitalization.

We are also called to serve the wider society, and we do so in the places where we work and in our various forms of witness and our work for justice.

Service is intrinsic to who we are and how we are to live. But the pressing question is: how can we find joy in our serving? Much serving may be done out of the drudgery of duty and the emptiness of our lives and hearts. Yet clearly this is not sustainable!

Thus we need to find deeper wells from which to drink. Service and prayer must inform one another. Action must emerge from contemplation. Our service must not be the product of our idealism, but rather be led by the Spirit. We need to overcome our messianic impulses and compulsions and serve within the acknowledged limitations of who we are and what we can do.

In this way, our joy will come not from our successes, but from knowing that we are doing what God asks of us.

SERVING: THE JOY OF SELF-GIVING

10.1 *Birthing*

We are all involved in the common activities of maintaining life: caring for family members, cleaning, washing, cooking, repairing, gardening, and so on. Many of these everyday tasks are often done in a hurry because we have "more important" things to do, yet we can choose to tend these ordinary things with mindfulness and joy. Much of our lives are also devoted to the domain of our paid occupations. In our paid work, we are doing more than maintaining our life-style. Hopefully, we see our work as a way of sustaining our life, contributing to the common good, and so living to the glory of God. Many of us also volunteer to help and encourage others who are in difficult circumstances and need our support. We operate variously in these three spheres, and we must not neglect one or the other. Moreover, as Christians, we are called to serve in all three spheres with a spirit of love, care and joy.

Yet St. Francis suggests that in all of our activity, we are to give birth to Christ. Just as the Word becoming flesh was the first and most fundamental incarnation, so Christ needs to be revealed in all the things we do: our cooking, our paid job, and our helping neighbours in need.

St. Francis writes "we are spouses" when we are united to Christ by faith through the Spirit; we are "mothers when we carry Him in our heart and body" and "give Him birth through holy activity."[1] Though Francis speaks of holy activity, he does not mean only religious activity. For any activity is holy if it is done in the spirit of Christ, in prayer, and in loving service to the other. All activity becomes holy if it is done to the glory of God.

This metaphor to bring Christ to birth in all we seek to do is powerful, but what does it mean? Certainly there is not a repetition of the first incarnation, but rather Christ becomes manifest and is spiritually present in all we do. This manifestation is multi-dimensional, for Christ is *in* the one who serves in his name and power. Moreover, Christ is *in* the act of serving, because Christ chooses to dwell in acts of love, care and nurture. Furthermore, Christ is *in* the one who is being served, regardless of who that person may be or what that person may believe or not believe. Christ is a hidden presence within each person, and all acts of witness and service invite the hidden Christ to come forth.

Yet bringing Christ to birth in all we do is not only a matter of manifestation, but also of transformation. Bringing Christ to birth in our family, church, or business is not simply about experiencing occasional flashes of light and inspiration from Christ's presence, but more about Christ gestating—taking shape and form—within our relationships and institutions. Thus our family, church and business take

SERVING: THE JOY OF SELF-GIVING

on the spirit of Christ; they take on Christ's values and function in the way of Christ. In this way, Christ is embodied within them.

Clearly we want to see this embodiment not only in the family, nor only the community of faith, nor only in friendships, but also in other arenas of life. So what does the gestalt of Christ look like in our prison system, our educational institutions, the business world and other spheres of society? When we give birth to Christ, it is not simply inward and personal, but also social.

Reflection

St. Patrick reminds us how much we need
God for all of this:
"I arise today through God's strength to pilot me,
God's might to uphold me,
God's wisdom to guide me."[2]

10.2 *In the Midst of Life*

In all religious traditions, there is a recognition that those who serve the spiritual needs of people in the church, mosque or temple are fulfilling an important service. But this form of service is not more important than those who live out their faith in the daily activities of life and in ordinary work.

St. John Chrysostom recognized that lay people were not only true servants of God, but needed special support as they lived a life of prayer and work amidst daily life. He writes: "You stand continuously in the front rank, you receive continual blows. So you need more remedies."[3] Chrysostom recognizes that those who serve in the sanctuary are not only there to serve God, but also to serve the people who are carrying their faith into daily life. One way to serve in this way is to form and empower people for their roles and tasks in the world.

Chrysostom believes that the task of Christians in the world is challenging and comprehensive. He notes: "Christians are the saviours of the city…they are its guardians, its patrons and its teachers."[4] While this may sound elitist and arrogant, we may understand Chrysostom by noting the following.

First, Christians are invited to be a praying presence amidst their life setting. Their prayers are not only for themselves and the faith community, but also for the well-being of the world. Christians pray for peace, good governance, the up-building of the common good and for justice to prevail.

Secondly, Christians are to be an example in the way they live and serve. They not only pray for the common good, but they help facilitate human flourishing through sacrificial service, the building of community, the creation of meaningful work, and nurturing social institutions that benefit all.

Thirdly, through prayer and action, Christians may well find themselves in circumstances where they are able to encourage and teach others. Seeing how they live, love, pray and serve, others may be attracted and want to learn something of this way of life.

In the contemporary Western world, where the church is generally not well respected, this poses a huge challenge. Yet this is the starting point for the church: to become more truly what God has provided it can be in the grace of Christ and the power of the Spirit.

Reflection

In faithfulness to the purposes of God
and in its task in the world,
the church is called to fullness of life in Christ
so that it may bless a neighbourhood, city, nation.

10.3 *Motivation in Service*

What motivates us is as important as what we do. Acts of kindness, generosity and the work for justice must come from a good place within us. We don't serve well from places of guilt, self-seeking or the misuse of power.

Thomas à Kempis is motivated by an inner humility that rejoices in the way God wants to use him: "To serve You does not seem so special to me, rather, what is outstanding and marvelous is that You have chosen one so pitiable and unworthy for your service and have numbered him [her] among Your beloved servants."[5] Such a humble attitude safeguards us against taking centre stage in serving God. It keeps us dependent on God's work in and through us, and it keeps us grateful for what God is doing.

Meister Eckhart reminds us that service is not to be a subtle form of self-aggrandizement: "Do all you can in the way of good works, solely for the praise of God." He continues: "You shall not ask anything in return for it and then your efforts will be both spiritual and divine."[6] Thus service is pure self-giving with an open hand that keeps no accounts.

The unknown author of *The Cloud of Unknowing* draws us into a deeper understanding of what should motivate us in serving others: "That which I am and the way that I am, with all my gifts of nature and grace, you have given to me,

SERVING: THE JOY OF SELF-GIVING

O Lord, and you are all of this. I offer it all to you principally to praise you and to help my fellow Christians and myself."[7] Thus while it is easy to give what we possess to others, particularly out of our excess, our primary call is to give of ourselves.

There are several important dimensions in this statement. First, who I am is sheer gift, forged by my upbringing and socialization and by the work of grace and the empowerment of the Spirit. As gift, I give myself back to God, who calls me to serve others with what God has shaped and enabled and gifted me to be.

A deeper dimension to giving of ourselves is that while we are called to serve God and our sisters and brothers in the faith, we don't serve those who are part of the Christian community exclusively. For we are called to serve the stranger as we would members of the faith community. Maximus the Confessor writes: "The one who imitates God by giving alms knows no difference between...[the] just and [the] unjust." He continues: the Christian "distributes to all without distinction according to their need."[8]

But the call to give of ourselves poses an even deeper challenge to our contemporary default mode of claiming that we possess what we have and can choose to share what we wish. This, of course, puts us in the driver's seat, where we are in control. Yet we are not possessors, but stewards. The ancient wisdom of the church has much to say about this. St. Clement writes: "All things therefore are common, and not for the rich to appropriate an undue share."[9] St. Ambrose (c.339–397), the fiery bishop of Milan, reminds us: "The earth was established as a common [patrimony] for all, for both rich and poor alike."[10] St. Cyril of Alexandria reiterates: "It [our wealth] does not belong to us…it truly belongs to the poor."[11] Chrysostom makes all of this clear: "Wealth is not a possession, it is not property; it is a loan for use."[12] And St. Basil brings home the challenge: "To the hungry belongs the bread that you keep….To the needy belongs the cash you hide away."[13]

In light of these challenges, one motivation that needs to grow in us is that we don't share what is ours. We merely pass on to others what has been entrusted to us.

In our materialistic age, where we see ourselves as the possessors of things, we are being invited by this ancient wisdom to live according to this new vision. Such a deep conversion will make us servants of God's reign, and this could change our world.

Reflection

From having to not-having and sharing
calls for a great transformation.

10.4 *Mentoring*

There are many ways we can serve others. We can certainly help people who are in need. And we can also be willing to get alongside of others to act as encourager and guide.

In the long history of Christian spirituality, one form this has taken is to be a spiritual director or companion for those who seek encouragement in the journey of faith.

In Celtic spirituality, Diarmuid O'Laoghaire points out: "No doubt the practice of *anamchairdeas,* spiritual direction, literally 'soul-friendship,' exercised by the *anamchara* or 'soul-friend'—also for lay people—was a great help towards fervor of life and the promotion of private penance and confession."[14]

In the monastic tradition, spiritual companioning was an important dimension in Christian formation. St. Basil writes that we need a person "who may serve you as a very sure guide in the work of leading a holy life." He continues that such a person must know "the straight road to God."[15]

Walter Hilton (d. 1396), the English mystic, Augustinian canon and head of the Priory at Thurgarton, makes a similar point: "If not even the least of the arts can be learned without some teacher and instructor how much more difficult it is to acquire the Art of Arts, the perfect service of God in the spiritual life, without a guide."[16]

The ancient wisdom is full of such admonitions. And we would do well to hear their advice and to prepare ourselves for such a service to others. So we should ponder: what does it take to be such a guide? And how can I serve others in this way?

To be a spiritual companion to others means that one has grown in spiritual wisdom and maturity to the point that one most deeply longs to see others flourish in their spiritual journey. This means that the companion has gone through many purgations in the move from self-interest to other-regarding.

It means that the companion does not seek to control, fix or advise. The companion is not messianic, nor is the companion interested in the inner life of another for curiosity's sake. Rather, the companion seeks to be an assistant to the Holy Spirit. The companion is interested in the well-being of the other and what the Spirit is doing in his or her life. The companion seeks to be co-discerner with the one coming for direction regarding the movement of the sustaining, transforming and life-giving work of the Spirit of God in the particularity of that person's life and journey.

Part of the task of spiritual direction is to provide a safe place for the directee to share something of his or her story. The companion is to hold all the elements of what the directee shares and to facilitate a reflective process. The task

SERVING: THE JOY OF SELF-GIVING

of spiritual direction is not so much to discern what God is saying on the spiritual mountaintop, since such a revelation is usually all too clear. Instead, the task is to co-discern the movement of the Spirit in the ordinariness of life and in the places of desolation and difficulty.

The need to serve others in this way is all too obvious. With limited participation in the faith community, with little formation in the Christian faith, with an overwhelming sense that we have to make our own way in life, with busy lives and demanding jobs, and with the sense that God often seems so far away, we need fellow travelers on this rocky road.

And while we may need the medical practitioner, the psychologist and life-skills mentor to help us in life's journey, we also need a spiritual guide. In the great discovery of being loved in the love of God in Christ and being gifted with the renewing and empowering Spirit, we need to live more deeply into all that God seeks to be for us.

Reflection

St. Patrick's prayer guides us:
"I arise today through God's strength to pilot me;
God's might to uphold me,
God's wisdom to guide me."[17]

10.5 *Joy in Service*

At first glance, we might think that it's impossible to find joy in service. For isn't service about self-giving—and isn't self-giving arduous? Doesn't service drain our energies? Of course! Giving ourselves to others is costly and calls for sacrifice.

Yet Hildegard of Bingen suggests that there is more to service than hard work: the one "who strongly does the good he [she] ardently desires" in the light of the divine command "shall dance in the true exultation of the joy of salvation."[18] This is an interesting challenge, for she is not describing someone simply doing his or her own thing, but rather someone acting in the light of God's will and purposes. To do things in the light of God's command, our hearts must be seeking to please and honour God, and we must be willing to be guided by God's wisdom.

Moreover, Hildegard suggests that this service comes from a deep and passionate internal desire, for she is not describing a reluctant obedience nor a grudging, half-hearted response to an external authority. Rather, this person has internalized the concerns of the gospel.

Such an inner transformation suggests a unitive experience, where what God wants is what I want, and what I want pleases God. Thus union with God, or being one with God, does not simply take place in inward reflection or prayer or in a contemplative experience. Being one with God is also possible in the midst of service. Our action and service join us to God as much as our prayer life.

Little wonder that this is the setting for joy. If I can live my heartfelt passions and concerns—the things that I deeply care about as I act into the world—and at the same time please God, then my service is both God-breathed and personally motivated. How good is this? It is wonderful! It is life-giving! And it is as empowering for me as it is for those I seek to serve.

Franciscan spirituality points us in a similar direction, as it gives us the vision of a unitive experience marked by joy. This has to do with the blessing of receiving Christ, of Christ being formed in us, and of our seeking to serve others out of the love of Christ within us. Put in other words, when I serve others in the way of Christ, then I meet Christ in the very act of service. In my act of self-giving, I meet again the self-giving Christ.

So the joy I may experience in service, no matter how light or sacrificial, has nothing to do with the success of what I seek to do on behalf of another. It is not a joy based on good outcomes. I may at this point see no fruit in my service, but I may experience great joy. And what constitutes this joy? It is the joy of knowing that I did what I felt

I must do. Thus there is the joy of obedience. But there is also the joy of meeting with my God in the act of service and of God being there with his Spirit. It is meeting with the hidden Christ in the face of the other. It is the joy of being allowed to serve God. It is the joy of being part of God's purposes for humanity. And yes, there is the joy of seeing someone blessed, of seeing a community slowly but surely transformed, of seeing someone grow in wholeness and of seeing a people grow in hope.

What most impacts others may not be what we give and do, but rather the spirit in which we act and serve. For if our service is an encounter with the presence of God, then something more than our actions are in play. So let us offer our service as an act of worship and an expression of great joy.

Reflection

Bonaventure prays:
"Let my mind meditate on this joy, my tongue speak of it,
My heart desire it, my words extol it,
My soul hunger for it, my flesh thirst for it…
Until I enter into the joy of my God."[19]

11

MOURNING:

Grieving Loss

The experience of loss is integral to the human story, a reality from which no one escapes. We can experience the loss of something we have or possess, such as investments, property or other possessions. We can lose these things as a result of the risks we take, or the bad choices we make, or because others fail us in some way, or because of things that are completely out of human control, such as war, natural disasters and other calamities.

At a much deeper level, we can experience the loss of loved ones, whether family, brothers and sisters in the faith or friends. When this loss is marked by tragedy—an accident, a virulent illness, suicide—our experience of loss is all the greater. We are deeply marked, forever changed—and some are destroyed—by such tragedies.

At a more insidious level, most of us experience the loss of quality in our relationships. Whether in marriage or friendship, with work colleagues or neighbours, what started well begins to lose its shine and go sour over time. Misunderstandings and woundings make us defensive, and we build barriers to protect ourselves, thus losing the companionship we once had.

We can also lose an opportunity that never returns or some aspect of our identity that can never be regained. We can lose confidence, direction, hope, and faith. Life's purpose can slip through our fingers.

Sadly, the experience of loss often triggers a domino effect. For if we lose our home, then we also lose our neighbours, and we may well lose our community of faith. A marriage breakdown or the severing of a significant partnership usually means the loss of place and other resources as well.

Amidst the turmoil of loss, we usually lash out at someone—it may be the one we see as the perpetrator, or we may blame ourselves and practice self-harm, or we may blame God for not preventing the tragedy and loss. But sooner or later, we need to move from anger to acceptance and so embrace what has come our way. This journey opens up possibilities for healing and renewed grace.

Thus through loss, we are invited to embark on a journey towards deeper self-insight, where we might sense a call to live differently in relation to our possessions or to establish new priorities. When we are willing to make this journey, our loss is transformed into an unexpected gift and a blessing in disguise. From out of our darkness moments, some light begins to shine.

MOURNING: GRIEVING LOSS

Loss is an important theme in the history of Christian spirituality. From our loss of connectedness with God and the call to homecoming and reconciliation flows the challenge to let go of the things we cling to in order to follow Christ and to be more fully conformed to his image. This draws us into the mysterious workings of God, where some things are taken away from us as an act of God's severe mercy. This is the hard road of purgation, where we are called to trust the One who wounds us. Hosea knew something about this and proclaims: "Come, let us return to the Lord; for it is he who has torn, and he will heal us; he has struck down, and he will bind us up" (Hosea 6:1).

We may be called to walk the empty road, to inhabit the dark places and to abide in the desert, where we lose all that is familiar in our Christian journey thus far. St. John of the Cross calls this the dark night of the soul, where we enter our own Gethsemane, which may well culminate in the cry on the cross: "Why, have you forsaken me?"

Yet the gospel also invites us to embrace the pathway of relinquishment as we surrender our very lives, through the grace of God, for the sake of the Kingdom of God. This is the journey towards an ascetic spirituality, not in order to gain kudos with God, but to be more attentive to God's ways and God's purposes with us so that God's will may be done on earth as in heaven.

IN THE FOOTSTEPS

11.1 *Mourning our Exile*

With the collapse of Christendom—the time when Christianity was a powerful social force and Church and State mutually reinforced each other—the church in the West as well as other parts of the world must navigate the new waters of this difficult and challenging interim state. The challenge before us is how to live our faith well from a position of marginality and how to trust God when there is so much uncertainty and fragility. How can we sustain a communal dark night of the soul? How do we maintain hope in the face of abandonment? How do we sing the Lord's song in a strange land? How can we shape our world from a position of weakness? In this time of great questioning and searching, there are countless pressing questions we will face as we continue along our unique journeys of faith.

In grappling with these questions, two ancient voices can guide us. First, Thomas à Kempis reminds us that "sometimes it is to our advantage to endure misfortunes and adversities for they make us enter into our inner selves and acknowledge that we are in a place of exile and that we ought not to rely on anything in this world."[1] Instead of reacting outwardly in times of challenge, Kempis invites us to move towards inner reflection, where we can embrace our pain and loss and acknowledge our vulnerabilities. From this posture, we can

MOURNING: GRIEVING LOSS

see more clearly how our very lives depend on God rather than ourselves and our circumstances.

Second, St. Anselm confesses: "I weep over the hardship of exile, hoping in the consolation of your coming, ardently longing for the glorious contemplation of your face."[2] Here we are called into the art of grieving. While Anselm may be longing for the final vision of God in the life to come, we most certainly need a revelation of God in the dark and difficult places of our earthly pilgrimage.

In facing the challenges before us, we must also relinquish our longings for the good old days, when things were better and the church was more powerful. We must accept the present marginalization of the church, live where we are and walk the road before us.

Yet how can we walk the present road with courage and faith, guided by the Spirit, when we feel as if we are being led into the desert rather than the promised land? This is the place of purgation, where we choose to trust God even in a dark and difficult place. In this place, where so much seems to be stripped away, we are called to make our own path by walking it. And though there are no clear signposts ahead of us, the ever-brooding Spirit is with us.

In this place of desolation and forsakenness, we mourn and raise our voices in lament, seeking the God on the road, not only the God of the sanctuary. We seek the God of the dark places, not only the God of dazzling light. We seek the God of the silences, not only the God who speaks. We seek the God of the lonely places, not only the God of community.

As we walk this road, we must not withdraw into our religious ghettoes. This is not a time for self-protection or isolation. Rather, this is a wonderful opportunity to engage our world from a place of prayer, humility, weakness and costly service rather than our previous position of strength.

Reflection

The unknown writer of
The Cloud of Unknowing reminds us:
"Now it is enough to worship God perfectly with your substance, that is, with the offering of your naked self."[3]

MOURNING: GRIEVING LOSS

11.2 *Mourning the Loss of Our Image of God*

One often hears within the faith community that while everything around us changes, God does not change. While this well-intended platitude is meant to encourage us to trust in God's steadfast love and faithfulness, it is hardly a sustainable proposition, no matter how attractive it may be from a pastoral point of view.

For even if we leave aside the idea that God does not change—and the incarnation clearly signals some change—our relationship with God is hardly a static reality. And God's relationship with us also features the dynamics of change. We cannot say that the world changes and we change—thereby signaling the insecurities of our existence—and at the same time say that the things of God do not change, thereby providing us with permanency and security.

To put this in the sharpest of terms, our relationship with God may be—and often is—just as fragile, uncertain and insecure as the rest of our relationships. If this is so, then the whole of our life is marked by vulnerability and fragility, including the spiritual dimensions of life.

This is good thing rather than a tragedy, for it means that in everything and in every way, we are called to live by faith. It means that the spiritual life is a pilgrimage. It means that our relationship with God is by its very nature dynamic. It means that we can't control God. In this way, we overcome every form of dualism that has plagued the church in its long journey in history, for this dualism has suggested that there is something inviolably permanent in us, e.g. our spirit.

There are at least three levels in which our relationship with God and God's relationship with us may change. First, at the broad level, changes in society and in our reading of Scripture can bring about such change. In an earlier world, God was seen as King, an earthly king was seen as God's representative, and we were to be subject both to God and the king as loyal subjects. In a democratic world, this scenario no longer works.

At the more personal level, our understandings of God may change over the course of the human life cycle. As a consequence, our relationship with God also changes. In our youth, we may have seen God in more activist terms. This God, with our help, was going to change the world and make right every wrong. In later life, one may see God differently. One may speak of the weakness of God in God's long-suffering of the stupidities of our lives and world.

Other changes may also occur. We may move from an understanding of God shaped by a domineering or absent father to understanding God in his great gentleness, generosity and faithful presence. Or we may cease seeing God in purely masculine terms as we begin to see God as beyond gender. As a result, we may see God, by way of human analogy, as both our father and mother.

This all points to the fact that we tend to have one-sided understandings of God, and we need to be drawn into a much more spacious place. Yet not only does our understanding of God change over time, but God also changes in relation to us. A common refrain in Scripture is that God hides from us, as in the psalmist's poignant cry: "How long, O Lord? Will you hide yourself forever?" (Psalm 89:46). Meister Eckhart notes that God "is a hidden God" and goes on to make the surprising comment, "The more one seeks Thee, the less one can find Thee."[4]

As we seek this "hidden" God, we are called to relinquish what we think we know of God to embrace the mystery of God's ways. We are also called to relinquish a sense of God's presence so that we can live by faith more deeply, without trying to "get God back" by our piety or activism.

This leads us to the hardest dimension of all in the Christian journey, the call to wait *on* God. The Psalmist knows this well: "Be still before the Lord, and wait patiently for him" (Psalm 37:7).

Reflection

St. Anselm's prayer:
"My consoler, for whom I wait. When will you come?
O…that I might be satisfied with the appearing
of your glory, for which I hunger."[5]

MOURNING: GRIEVING LOSS

11.3 *Embracing Our Grief and Sorrow*

There is little doubt that we give grief to others when we disappoint and fail them. No one avoids this difficult pathway, for we can never live up to others' expectations for us, and we can never be all we would like to be in relation to others.

We also grieve the heart of God. The Psalmist gives us this sad generalization about the people of Israel: "How often they rebelled against him [Yahweh] in the wilderness and grieved him in the desert" (Psalm 78:40). And Jesus is described in Mark's gospel at being distressed about the Pharisees' lack of compassion for people in need: "He [Jesus] looked around at them with anger; he was grieved at their hardness of heart" (Mark 3:5).

And we also grieve both our losses and our own failures. We grieve what we could have done or said, but did not. We grieve the fact that we hurt others. We grieve our own lack of growth in the spiritual life. And we grieve the state of the church and the world. Indeed, there is much to grieve about!

While failure and loss is not good, grieving and mourning is good, for it puts us in touch with the pain and disappointment within us and helps us move forward. People who know how to grieve are people who can be honest with themselves and others. In giving advice to another Christian St. Jerome admits: "I am no experienced mariner who has never lost either ship or cargo."[6] St. Augustine, in reflecting on his life, notes: "I vacillated and thou guided me. I roamed the broad way of the world, and thou didst not desert me."[7]

Those who mourn and grieve are not locked into the pain and disappointments of the past, stuck in the valley of despair, for they have embraced their losses and traversed their dark places. Freed to move forward, they will move forward in a different way. For like Jacob of old, they now have a limp and have become wounded healers. They have been bruised, but have gained a gentle wisdom.

But at a much deeper level, we also continually mourn our general human condition, with our loss of the garden of Eden and our pristine relationship with God. St. Anselm alludes to this in his heart cry: "Refashion the face I that I have spoiled, restore the innocence that I have violated."[8] What folly that our forebears forfeited the garden, and what greater folly that we have followed in their footsteps. And what greater madness that we have refused the God who seeks us out for full restoration!

But even if we turn towards God and embrace the salvation offered in Christ and open our lives to the brooding, life-giving Spirit, we are not beyond grief. For now our grief is deepened as we mourn our sojourn here and long for our

MOURNING: GRIEVING LOSS

final homecoming. Thus our pilgrim status is a journey of lament as well as joy. St. Augustine confesses: "As for myself, I will enter into my closet and there sing to thee the songs of love, groaning with groanings that are unutterable now in my pilgrimage."[9]

For the object of our love, God himself, is still so far from us, and the consummation of all things still lies in the mists of the future. Our final homecoming will first lead us through the valley of death. Hadewijch of Antwerp, the thirteenth-century Dutch Beguine and mystic, says poetically: "More multitudinous than the stars of heaven are the griefs of love."[10]

Reflection

Hadewijch invites us to embrace the pilgrim
status of the Christian journey.
She proposes that we find grace for a
"fidelity that allows itself to rest peacefully without
the full possession of Love [God]."[11]

11.4 *Mourning Our Lack of Vision*

The grace of God in Christ is the power that can free us from sin's dominion and liberate us from the wounding and mistakes of our past. This power can compel us to live into the future with hope and courage and empower us with the life-giving Spirit. It can also draw us into the heart and purposes of God for the renewing of all things.

Little wonder that the apostle Paul celebrates this: "So if anyone is in Christ, there is a new creation: everything old has passed away; see, everything has become new!" (2 Corinthians 5:17). And elsewhere he proclaims: "For neither circumcision nor uncircumcision is anything; but a new creation is everything!" (Galatians 6:15).

Yet as the old within us drags on, we seem to fall far short of this grand vision. We are still so culture bound. Past hurts and mistakes continue to plague us. Unbelief mingles with bursts of great faith. Our single-mindedness frequently erodes in the wash of fickleness and uncertainty. We seem to be a divided self rather than the new creation that Paul pictures for us.

Thus we mourn the gap between what we are and what Christ calls us to be. And we grieve our lack of vision, for vision is birthed in who we are becoming through the grace of God and the power of the Spirit.

MOURNING: GRIEVING LOSS

But perhaps our hope does not lie in where we are and who we have already become, but rather in who Christ is and what Christ has gained for us. And maybe our capacity does not lie in our own strength, but rather in our weakness.

The Medieval mystic Marguerite Porete confesses: "Lord, how much do I comprehend of your power, of your wisdom, and of your goodness? As much as I comprehend of my own weakness, of my foolishness, and of my wickedness."[12]

Paul also emphasizes this when he writes: "For whenever I am weak, then I am strong" (2 Corinthians 12:10). Paul is so convinced of this upside-down wisdom that he applies it to the work of God. In speaking about God's strange way of salvation through the crucifixion of Christ, he testifies: "For God's foolishness is wiser than human wisdom, and God's weakness is stronger than human strength" (1 Corinthians 1:25).

This opens up a new pathway for us. For when we fail to be who we long to be in Christ, we are drawn to seek the face of God. Our very lack of vision guides us to seek the wisdom of God. When we mourn our present capacity, we open ourselves to receive the grace of God. As we grope towards the light, we are already receiving more light than we may realize. Thus it is through humility and vulnerability—rather than piety—that we receive the vision of God. For vision is always a gift, never our possession.

As such, we may receive a very simple or a very grand vision. St. Isaac the Syrian had a grand vision. He speaks of "a heart aflame with love for the entire creation, for people, birds, beasts, evil spirits, all creatures…moved by an infinite pity that is awakened in the hearts of those who resemble God."[13]

Julian of Norwich had a much simpler vision, though possibly equally grand. In speaking of a hazelnut she says, "God made it…God loves it…God preserves it." In this way she had a vision of God as "the creator…protector and the lover."[14]

And St. Benedict puts it all so simply when he writes: "Your way of acting should be different from the world's way; the love of Christ must come before all else."[15]

Whatever vision God gives us, we are to receive in faith. We are not to create our own vision, for God will only enable and empower what is given and received through grace. To live that vision well will take the whole of our lives.

Reflection

Hildegard of Bingen speaks of patriarchs and prophets,
"who traversed the hidden ways of God
and looked with the eyes of the spirit."
In "lucent shadows [they] announced the Living Light."[16]

11.5 *Misplaced Grief*

When we experience loss, the grief that follows is appropriate. But we can also grieve the loss of things from which we should really rejoice to be free.

It is not at all appropriate to grieve when an illegal business deal fails, or when we gamble on the wrong horse, or when an inappropriate relationship comes to an end. In these instances, it is more appropriate to confess our wrongdoing and grieve our willfulness and stupidity.

In the frame of Christian spirituality, we can misplace our grief when we fear that in following God's way we are going to lose what we have or what is dear to us. At the deepest level, we fear that we will lose our very selves.

Much of this fear is fanned into flame when we focus on the heroes and martyrs of the ancient church, as well as Mahatma Gandhi, Dietrich Bonhoeffer, Martin Luther King, Jr. and Oscar Romero from our modern times. In these martyrs, we see the outworking of the cost of discipleship—which they paid with their very lives.

This spawns a host of questions. Is God really a demanding God? Does God only take away what is bad in our lives, or does God also take away what is good? Does God want all of us so that we lose ourselves? Does God only confront our false selves or also our real selves?

The language of ancient wisdom suggests a loss of self as we become lost in God. St. Columbanus writes: "Let Christ paint his own image in us."[17] St. Bernard of Clairvaux takes this a step further: we are to merge into God like "a drop of water…disappear[ing] completely in a quantity of wine." He continues: "It is necessary for human affection to dissolve in some ineffable way and be poured into the will of God."[18] And the Medieval mystic, Jan van Ruysbroeck, puts this most clearly: "All our powers then fail us and we fall down in open contemplation. All become one and one becomes all in the loving embrace of the threefold unity. When we experience this unity, we become one being, one life, and one blessedness with God."[19]

While this language may suggest a loss of self, the focus is on a spiritual union with God as we become more conformed to the image of Christ. As we become more godly, we become more truly who God created us to be. Thus we become our true selves.

Rather than being absorbed into God and thereby losing ourselves, our true selves are healed and renewed. We are restored, not negated. One of the Desert Fathers puts this most simply: "Tell me, beloved, if thy cloak were torn, wouldst [thou] throw it away?" He continues: "Nay, but I would patch it." He then concludes: "If thou wouldst spare thy garment, shall not God have mercy on His own image?"[20]

MOURNING: GRIEVING LOSS

God's renewing work is to place us in the domain of freedom so that we can do God's will. St. Anselm puts this well: "By you the world is renewed and made beautiful with truth…By you sinful humanity is justified, the condemned are saved, the servants of hell are set free."[21] And St. Cyril of Alexandria puts it even more clearly: "Christ is for us a pattern and beginning and image of the divine way of life, and he displayed clearly how and in what manner it is fitting for us to live."[22]

Thus we aren't to mourn the loss of ourselves, for God does not destroy his beloved creation. When we yield to the God who remakes us, we embrace God's healing activity in our lives and foster God's friendship. When we embrace rather than fear what God asks of us, we are beckoned into God's purposes for our world. As we embark on this pilgrimage, God will make us whole and sustain us along the way. Food and wine for the journey have already been provided.

Reflection

Florentius Radewijns (1350–1400), one of the leaders of
the Brethren of the Common Life, reminds us: our
"final destination is the Kingdom of God."
"The road that leads to that goal is purity of heart."
And "woe to the knowledge that
does not turn to loving."[23]

12

WAITING:

Living in Expectation

In an older world waiting was a given. One could wait for years to hear from someone who had moved to another part of the then-known world. In that world one was also much more dependent on the cycles of nature. The mother waited for news from her son. The farmer waited for good weather and a good harvest.

Waiting is no longer a given in our world, where we have instant communication and expect instant results. Rather than waiting, we are constantly trying to make things happen.

Unlike the spirituality of our ancient forebears, who waited in the tradition of the Desert Fathers and Mothers and monastic communities, we moderns know little of a spiritual waiting. Ours is an impatient spirituality. We are restless with a God who is far too slow for us and a Spirit who has become moribund.

Thus we have a self-made spirituality. We make church happen with our slick programs. We drown out silence from the sanctuary. We make mission happen with our activism. And we are constantly wondering why God is not keeping up with all we are seeking to do.

One sign of this is that our prayer life is pragmatic and minimalistic. Our retreats are seminars. The spiritual disciplines are seen as outdated and meditative practices are consigned to the elderly or those recovering from some major crisis.

We know how to justify this. For why wait for God when God has made us vice-regents in his world? Why wait for God when God has made us co-belligerents in his purposes? Why wait to pray when we have the Spirit to lead us? Why wait to reflect or meditate when we are supposed to be the hands and feet of Jesus?

In spite of our justifications, there are many reasons that compel us to recover a spirituality of waiting. First, waiting is part of the biblical narrative, which should shape the contours of the Christian life. Secondly, waiting on God gives God his rightful place and acknowledges our vulnerability and need. In waiting we acknowledge that God is God and we are not. Thirdly, waiting on God purges us from our own compulsions and self-aggrandizement. So much of what we do, while seemingly good, does not spring from the leading of the Spirit. Fourthly, waiting on God draws us into the pathways of prayer and reflection that need to undergird all we seek to do in the service of the Reign of God. This integrates prayer and work and work and prayer.

In the Old Testament, waiting is an important theme. The Israelites waited long for their Egyptian deliverance and for their return from exile. They waited for the glory of Yahweh to fill the earth. And even today they wait for the Messiah to come. The psalms speak often of this waiting: "For God alone my soul waits in silence; from him comes my salvation" (Psalm 62:1). "I wait for the Lord, my soul waits, and in his word I hope" (Psalm 130:5). "But those who wait for the Lord shall renew their strength" (Isaiah 40:31). "But as for me, I will look to the Lord, I will wait for the God of my salvation; my God will hear me" (Micah 7:7).

In the New Testament, waiting is also an important theme. The crowds regularly waited for Jesus (Luke 8:40), Joseph of Arimathea waited for the kingdom of God (Mark 15:43), Christians wait for their full adoption as sons and daughters of God (Romans 8:23), they wait for the hope of righteousness (Galatians 5:5), and they wait for the return of Christ (1 Thessalonians 1:10). As Christians, we wait for a just world, the salvation of all, the glory of God to be fully revealed, the return of Christ, the healing of the nations, and the blessedness of new heavens and a new earth.

At an individual level, we wait for God to draw near to us in prayer. We wait for God to reveal his purposes. We wait for blockages to be removed and for doors to open. We wait for our prayers to be answered—for our families to be blessed, for colleagues to come to faith, for the flourishing of the common good, for justice to blossom, for peace in our world and for God's future to break in upon us.

This is an active waiting. We wait for what God alone can do.

12.1 Waiting and Withdrawal

When we wait for someone to come, we look forward to spending time together. In our expectancy, our sense of aloneness may deepen, and so we become disappointed and frustrated if the other person does not show up. Yet this expectant waiting can be productive if we see our time alone as a gift for reflection. We could think about the friend we were expecting and give thanks for this person. We could use this down-time for prayer. Waiting for someone is a form of Sabbath spirituality.

In Christian spirituality, waiting is an important theme. When we wait for God, we acknowledge God's friendship and Lordship. We wait for God in quiet reflection because we seek God's companionship and presence. We wait for God in prayer because we are seeking God's direction for our lives. To wait in this way, we practice the art of withdrawal. St. Anselm speaks about this: "Free yourself awhile for God and rest awhile in him." He goes on: "Enter the inner chamber of your soul, shut everything out, except God."[1] Thomas à Kempis sounds a similar note: "Set aside an opportune time for deep personal reflection and think often about God's many benefits to you."[2]

While one can pray while working and being busy, what is the value of withdrawing from one daily activities in order to wait on God and to wait for God? To wait on God is a form of service to God. This not only involves the practices of stillness, solitude and attentiveness, but may also involve worship and thanksgiving. To wait on God is not only a form of gratitude, but a waiting to hear what God may say or do.

This is exemplified in the biblical story in a myriad of ways. Samuel prays, "Speak, Lord, for your servant is listening" (1 Samuel 3:9). Job confesses, "I had heard of you by the hearing of the ear, but now my eyes see you; therefore I despise myself, and repent in dust and ashes" (Job 42:5–6). The Psalmist also picks up this theme: "I bless the Lord who gives me counsel; in the night also my heart instructs me" (Psalm 16:7). And more specifically: "I wait for the Lord, my soul waits, and in his word do I hope" (Psalm 130:5).

As we wait on God, we move towards God in worship, prayer and listening, but as we wait, God also moves towards us. And we soon discover that God has a different timetable and works in ways that are often different from our expectations.

Sometimes, when we wait for God to guide us, God is silent. But in such long periods of silence, we often discover that we have been slowly transformed to be more open to whatever God may ask of us. As we ask God to reveal himself to our neighbour or friend, we may ourselves grow in the gift of charity and so begin to welcome the ones for whom we have been praying. As we seek God's face to bless the poor, over time we may be drawn more deeply into asceticism and generosity. Waiting for God, even when it might feel as if we are waiting for Godot, may well be one of the most productive moves that God makes towards us.

How strange that God's seeming inactivity can be transformational! This makes our waiting productive, so long as we don't give up and lose heart. After long silences fruitful with faithful prayer, God may act in astonishing ways: revival may come to the church, a Berlin wall may come down, a war may cease, the poor may be lifted out of the ash heaps of their lives, prophets may be raised up, and goodness may come to a society.

Reflection

In the words of St. Bernard of Clairvaux,
"Lift up the ears of your heart to hear this inner voice…
[it] is the voice of magnificence and
power rolling through the desert,
revealing secrets shaking souls free."[3]

12.2 *Waiting in the Spirit*

As we practice the difficult art of waiting, there are many postures we might take. Many of us wait with impatience, because God seems to be moving far too slowly. Like the sons of Zebedee we, too, would like to help things along by calling fire down from heaven (Luke 9:52–55). Such a strategy is for the zealous, who are often far ahead of God. Yet it is also possible to languish in our waiting, where hope fades and prayer dies. We begin to rationalize that we were mistaken in the direction we felt God calling us, so we put our hopes and dreams to bed to slumber into forgetfulness.

A more fruitful waiting will require clarity about what we are waiting for and a sense of God sustaining us in our waiting through the Spirit, who breathes hope and faith in us. Our waiting is not fulfilled through self-realization, but rather revelation. Hildegard of Bingen speaks of the patriarchs and prophets, "who traversed the hidden ways and looked with eyes of the spirit" and "in lucent shadows [they] announced the Living Light."[4] These prophets saw in faith what Simeon and Anna saw when Mary and Joseph brought the child Jesus to the temple. And Simeon and Anna saw a glimpse of the future ministry of Jesus. Simeon proclaimed: "This child is destined for the falling and rising of many in Israel, and to be sign that will be opposed so that the inner thoughts of many will be revealed—and a sword will pierce your own soul too," he said to Mary (Luke 2:34–35).

Both Simeon and Anna are icons of waiting with hope, faith and anticipation to see the Messiah. Nothing daunted them! Anna was already eighty-four years of age and had been waiting for most of her life. In Luke's gospel, Simeon is called "righteous and devout, looking for the consolation of Israel" (Luke 2:25). He was not looking for a personal blessing but for national redemption. His waiting had to do with a kingdom vision, the in-breaking of the Reign of God. Well before John the Baptist speaks of Jesus baptizing people with the Holy Spirit (Luke 3:16) and Jesus himself going forth in the power of the Spirit (Luke 4:1), Simeon—who fades completely from view in the rest of the gospel narrative—is a waiter, a seer, upon whom the Holy Spirit rests (Luke 2:25). "It had been revealed to him by the Holy Spirit that he would not see death before he had seen the Lord's Messiah" (Luke 2:26). Moreover, the Spirit guided him to be at the temple just at the time when Mary and Joseph brought Jesus to be circumcised (Luke 2:27). This pregnant waiting exemplifies a waiting on the Spirit, a waiting in faith that gives birth, a waiting that is sustained not simply by inward conviction, but by the breath of the Spirit.

St. Basil (c. 330–379), one of the Cappadocian Fathers, suggests that the work of the Spirit, while deeply personal, is not simply about personal piety and personal effectiveness, which seems to be the emphasis today. Rather, he sees the action of the Spirit as communal, global and cosmic. He writes: the Spirit is given "to everyone who receives It…[It is] given to him [her] alone…[It] sends forth grace sufficient and full for all mankind."[5] St. Basil then emphasizes how the Spirit carries us into the future in faith, for from the Spirit "comes foreknowledge of the future, understanding of mysteries, apprehension of what is hidden, distributions of good gifts." He then goes on to reflect the great dictum of Patristic theology, with its idea that God becomes human so that humans may become God, suggesting that the Spirit's work in us has to do with "being made God."[6]

However we may understand this union with God in the Spirit, clearly this waiting involves waiting on God, being upheld by God and sustained by the Spirit.

Reflection

To wait in hope is to be the bearers of a new world.

12.3 *Waiting without Striving*

In our contemporary world, we seem to be known for what we do and achieve. Thus our sense of self and self-worth is premised on our productiveness. In the older world, status was the fruit of one's inheritance, but in the modern world, status flowers from one's entrepreneurship. Given this context, we should not be surprised that striving has become the hallmark of our world.

While God calls us to the good labour of shaping and eliciting change in our world, stewarding creation and building the common good, so much of our striving is based on an unhealthy foundation. For rather than being oriented towards the common good, our focus is on self-enhancement and creating an identity through our achievements. This is an endless and hopeless quest, for our achievements will always lead to more striving, and this contributes to the great restlessness that plagues our world.

For a healthy identity is not created by our achievements but by being well loved. And being loved well is being loved with eyes of wonder and favour. God's smile of grace is more impacting than the long duty of religious scrupulousness. And parental loving acceptance and encouragement is more fruitful than a shaping of a child's identity through performance-based acceptance.

WAITING: LIVING IN EXPECTATION

But if striving is such an integral part of our present landscape, how do we enter the terrain of waiting? To expand on this territorial imagery, striving promises green pastures while waiting suggests the desert. But in reality, those promised green pastures are soon blighted by the fierce sun of unfulfilled expectations, while the desert brings forth unexpected blossoms. So how is waiting important for our sense of identity and well-being?

Our impulse to strive for achievements and accomplishments is based on insecurity and mistrust, while waiting is based on trust and hope. When I wait, I need to trust and believe that the other will come and do what is needed. Thus waiting is profoundly relational, hopeful and anticipatory. Being willing to wait also says something about our needs and limitations. Those who are powerful don't wait; they command. The restless don't wait; they worry. Achievers don't wait; they act. But the humble wait, because they know they can't do everything themselves; they know they need others.

Thus in the art of waiting, we are in a liminal space. We are in some sense powerless, but we are anticipating the one who is to come. So often this space can become the place of revelation, but it may also be a place of pruning and repentance.

In Christian spirituality, waiting is Sabbath time. Waiting is the dark Saturday that lies between Good Friday and

Easter Sunday. Waiting is the land lying fallow. Waiting is the long winter months for those living far away from the perpetual warmth of the equator.

Seasons of waiting are strange gifts that come to us in life's transitions, in loss, in re-location, in pilgrimage, and in the "dark night of the soul." But more fundamentally, waiting marks the fundamental gestalt of what it means to be a Christian. Thus waiting is neither a program nor a strategy, but rather an ontology of our very existence. When we wait well, we *are* well.

Those who know how to wait know that a meaningful life encompasses more than what they do. They know that life is what has been given and what is yet to come, and they are waiting for the fullness of God's Kingdom.

Reflection

St. Anselm says:
"My consoler for whom I wait, when will you come?
O that I might seek the joy that I desire;
that I might be satisfied with the appearing
of your glory for which I hunger."[7]

12.4 *Waiting for Justice*

Christians are called to wait and pray for the life to come: the return of Christ and the new heavens, new earth and whole new order of existence that his return will bring. Christians are also called to wait and pray and work for what may yet happen in this present world.

What many hope for in this life orbits around the themes of prayer and work. We pray and work for the Kingdom of God to come more fully amongst us. We pray and work for justice, for human flourishing and for a blossoming of the common good. But so often we think that this has nothing to do with waiting but only with action.

Though we work and strive for justice, we must also wait for it, because we cannot merely bring it about. If this were possible, then justice may have flourished in our world a long time ago. But in the face of injustice and oppression, justice is not won once and for all; it has to emerge.

The people in South Africa not only worked hard and prayed long for apartheid to be banished from their land, they also waited for it. Then a myriad of factors suddenly came together—a *kairos* moment! A confluence that no single person, movement or group could have orchestrated!

This waiting is never resigned, passive, cynical or hopeless. Rather, this waiting is active and hopeful in its anticipation that the right time will come. It came for Filipinos in the Edsa Revolution—a revolution where no gun was fired and not a life was lost. And it may yet come more fully for the Burmese as their country inches towards greater freedoms.

Waiting acknowledges that the quest for freedom, justice and shalom is bigger than all our best efforts. Change in our world depends on us, but it is also beyond us. Yet our most meager efforts may be a spark that lights the flame. Thus we work in hope. We pray in hope. And we wait in hope.

And we put our faith in the ongoing work of God in human affairs, a transcendent God who is both wholly Other and wholly concerned. This God is mindful of us all (Psalm 8). This God upholds all who fall and lifts up those who are downcast (Psalm 145:14). This God upholds the cause of the oppressed and sets prisoners free (Psalm 146:7). This God casts the proud to the ground and lifts up the humble (Psalm 147:5–6). And if this is the nature of God, then this should be the nature of our practice, prayer and waiting.

Our practice must start in the community of faith, for justice must be evident at home before it can be translated into the wider society. St. Ambrose writes: the church "pours the same grace not only upon the rich and mighty, but also upon men of low estate, she weighs them all in an equal balance, gathers them all into the same bosom, cherishes them in the same lap."[8]

The church is called to be a community of justice, welcome and empowerment—not simply in its teaching and preaching, but in the very nature of its life together. Yet the twenty-first century church has become so seduced by the values of our contemporary world that its prophetic witness has weakened. This is the greatest challenge facing the church today.

The church is to be a seed sown into the world. A seed is neither great nor powerful, but it does need to be authentic—a true seed of the Kingdom of God, a true reflection of the gospel, a true reflection of the way of Christ. Sadly, the church has not fully practiced this, still assuming that its influence lies in power, while it really rests in a seed that is willing to die.

Reflection

St. Benedict writes:
"Your way of acting should be different
from the world's way;
the love of Christ must come before all else."[9]

12.5 *For Those Who Wait*

Not everything we wait and hope for will eventually come our way. If we wait long enough, we will *not* eventually get what we hoped for. Time of itself is not the purveyor of good things. Certain things don't come about, some things are not given, and some things are taken away—this is all part of the human story.

While we may puzzle hard and long about why this is so, we may well have to bow before mystery and the ways of God beyond our understanding. We must also acknowledge the brokenness of the human condition. We sin and are sinned against—even by those most dear to us. And sometimes we need to recognize that what we had hoped for may not have been good for us.

While this can make us hard and bitter, it can also call us to live with deeper grace, surrender and gratitude. We grieve our disappointed hopes, and we choose to be thankful for what we do receive.

But in the long history of Christian spirituality, women and men of faith were not waiting for self-enhancement, benefits and blessings. Rather, they were waiting for God himself. St. Anselm writes: "My consoler, for whom I wait, when will you come? O that I might seek the joy that I desire; that I might be satisfied with the appearing of your glory for

WAITING: LIVING IN EXPECTATION

which I hunger; that I might be satisfied with the riches of your house for which I sigh."[10]

What is this kind of waiting all about? Why wait for the God we have already received? Why long for the God who has already drawn near? Why hunger when bread and wine have already been provided?

Though we may have received the presence of God into our lives, we long for more. Though God has moved in our lives, we wait for the further work of God within us. Though God has worked through the church, we hope for the church's renewal and empowerment. What we have seen by faith of God's action in our world stirs us to cry: God have mercy upon us and our world and renew the face of the earth, cause justice to flourish, wars to cease, and your shalom to envelop all.

We are to pray and act, but we are also invited to wait. We wait for the renewing work of the Spirit. We await the fuller presence of God. We wait for the Kingdom of God to be fully revealed. We wait for new heavens and a new earth. As we wait, St. Ambrose encourages us: "You received Him into the dwelling of your mind; you saw Him in spirit; you saw with inner eyes. Hold fast your new guest, long awaited, but lately received."[11] This inner revelation was preceded by a long time of waiting, and Ambrose invites his readers to cling to what has been given. In our age, when almost everything we could ever hope for is promised—including youth in old age—we are invited to wait, long for and cling to Someone else.

Reflection

> "My soul waits for the Lord
> more than those
> who watch for the morning,
> more than those
> who watch for the morning."[12]

Afterword

By looping back again and again to these ancient writings, I hope you have been refreshed and guided by their wisdom. I also hope you might be stirred to read these writings more fully, for these women's and men's lives of prayer, contemplation, community and service are beacons of light. Their faithfulness can inspire us and challenge us when we become enamored with the dominant values of contemporary culture.

Thus the ancient wisdom is meant to be a prophetic challenge to us in the twenty-first century. These reflections are meant not only to enrich us, but also to turn us around. As such, these ancient voices may come to us with a new vigour and freshness.

What is so wonderfully clear in the writings of our ancient forebears is that God was not an addendum. God was central. God was all. They sought God for God's-sake, for God's glory. And they believed that the more fully their lives were rooted in God, the more truly human they were. They saw their formation within their religious community as a reflection of the community of the Trinity, and they believed that living a Trinitarian life would sustain them and

AFTERWORD

empower them to serve the world. Their quest for God was not escapist, but integrative, weaving the presence of God into all of life.

The challenge facing contemporary Christianity is *not* the problem of its relevance to the world—we are so relevant that we are no longer distinctive. Rather, as Christians we need to become more fully what God has called us to be, that we might become a prophetic and healing presence in our world.

Endnotes

Chapter 1

1. Catherine of Genoa, *Purgation and Purgatory; The Spiritual Dialogue.* The Classics of Western Spirituality (London: SPCK, 1979), 30, 33.

2. Quoted in Malcolm Muggeridge, *A Third Testament* (Farmington: The Plough Publishing House, 2002), 15.

3. B. Ward, trans., *The Prayers and Meditations of Saint Anselm with the Proslogion* (London: Penguin Books, 1973), 181.

4. Two famous articulations of ladders of perfection were John Climacus' *Ladder of Divine Ascent* and Guigo II's *The Ladder of Monks.* See L. S. Cunningham & K. S. Egan, *Christian Spirituality: Themes from the Tradition* (New York: Paulist Press, 1996), 53.

5. F. J. Foster & J. B. Smith, eds., "Life and Teachings," in *Devotional Classics* (New York: Harper San Francisco, 1993), 212.

6. E. Spearing, ed., "The Mirror of Simple Souls," in *Medieval Writings on Female Spirituality* (New York: Penguin Books, 2002), 141.

ENDNOTES

7. See C. Williams, *John Wesley's Theology Today* (London: Epworth Press, 1969), 41-46.

8. W. Johnston, ed., *The Cloud of Unknowing and The Book of Privy Counseling* (Garden City: Image Books, 1973), 60.

9. R. B. Blakney, trans., *Meister Eckhart: A Modern Translation* (New York: Harper & Row, 1941), 34.

10. Thomas à Kempis, *The Imitation of Christ: In Four Books* (New York: Vintage Books,1998), 26.

11. Ibid., 83.

12. B. Ward, trans., *Prayers and Meditations of Saint Anselm,* 256.

13. R. C. Petry, ed., "The Mending of Life," in *Late Medieval Mysticism,* vol. 13 of *The Library of Christian Classics* (London: SCM Press, 1957), 238.

14. W. Johnston, ed., *The Cloud of Unknowing,* 155.

15. B. Ward, trans., *Prayers and Meditations of Saint Anselm,* 153.

16. E. Griffen, ed., *Hildegard of Bingen: Selections from Her Writings* (New York: Harper San Francisco, 2005), 129.

17. A. C. Outler, ed., *The Confessions of St. Augustine* (Mineola, N.Y.: Dover Publications, Inc., 2002), 252.

18. Helen Waddell, trans., *The Desert Fathers* (New York: Vintage Books, 1998), 68.

19. Quoted in D. J. Sheerin, *The Eucharist: Message of the Church Fathers,* vol. 17 (Wilmington: Michael Glazier, 1986), 322.

ENDNOTES

20. Quoted in A. Hyma, *The Brethren of the Common Life* (Grand Rapids: Eerdmans, 1950), 29.

21. R. B. Blakney, trans., *Meister Eckhart,* 239.

22. Quoted in Jean Leclercq, *The Love of Learning and the Desire for God* (New York: Fordham University Press, 1974), 284.

23. Quoted in Jean Leclercq, *The Love of Learning and the Desire for God,* 285.

Chapter 2

1. R. B. Blakney, trans., *Meister Eckhart,* 237.

2. Ibid., 15.

3. A. C. Outler, ed., *The Confessions of St. Augustine,* 90.

4. Ibid., 270.

5. Quoted in Rowan Williams, *Where God Happens: Discovering Christ in One Another* (Boston: New Seeds, 2005), 99.

6. Clifton Wolters, trans., Julian of Norwich, *Revelations of Divine Love* (London: Penguin Books, 1966), 207.

7. E. Griffin, ed., "On Conversion," in *Bernard of Clairvaux: Selected Works* (New York: Harper San Francisco, 2005), 26.

8. Quoted in Paul Evdokimov, *Ages of the Spiritual Life* (Crestwood: St. Vladimir's Seminary Press, 1998), 77.

9. Quoted in Jurgen Moltmann, *The Trinity and the Kingdom* (Minneapolis: Fortress Press, 1993), 14.

ENDNOTES

10. B. Ward, trans., *The Prayers and Meditations of Saint Anselm,* 130.

11. Quoted in I. Delio, *Franciscan Prayer* (Cincinnati: St. Anthony Messenger Press, 2004), 20.

12. O. Davies, trans., "Sermons of Columbanus," in *Celtic Spirituality, The Classics of Western Spirituality* (New York: Paulist Press, 1999), 358.

13. W. Johnston, ed., *The Cloud of Unknowing,* 156.

14. Thomas à Kempis, *The Imitation of Christ,* 36.

15. Quoted in A. Hyma, *The Brethren of the Common Life,* 31.

16. Quoted in P. Evdokimov, *Ages of the Spiritual Life,* 130.

17. W. Johnston, ed., *The Cloud of Unknowing,* 51.

18. R. J. Foster & J. B. Smith, eds., "Life and Teachings," in *Devotional Classics*, 213.

19. Helen Waddell, trans., *The Desert Fathers,* 155.

20. E. R. Hardy, "Address on Religious Instruction," in *Christology of the Later Fathers: The Library of Christian Classics* (Philadelphia: The Westminster Press, 1954), 56.

21. R. B. Blakney, trans., *Meister Eckhart,* 22.

22. J. J. O'Meara, trans., *Origen: Ancient Christian Writers,* no. 19 (New York: Newman Press, 1954), 125.

23. Quoted in P. Evdokimov, *Ages of the Spiritual Life,* 190.

24. Quoted in Simon Chan, *Spiritual Theology: A Systematic Study of the Christian Life* (Downers Grove: IVP, 1998), 181.

25. E. Griffin, ed., *Bernard of Clairvaux: Selected Works,* 128.

ENDNOTES

26. Thomas à Kempis, *The Imitation of Christ,* 108.

27. R. C. Petry, ed., "The Mending of Life," in *Late Medieval Mysticism,* vol. 13, 238.

28. B. Ward, trans., *The Prayers and Meditations of Saint Anselm,* 256.

29. R. J. Foster & J. B. Smith, eds., "Revelations of Divine Love," in *Devotional Classics*, 71.

30. Quoted in M. Fox, ed., *Western Spirituality: Historical Roots, Ecumenical Routes* (Santa Fe: Bear & Company, 1981), 229.

31. R. B. Blakney, trans., *Meister Eckhart,* 34.

Chapter 3

1. J. B. Shaw, trans., *St. Augustine: The Enchiridion on Faith, Hope and Love* (Washington: Regnery Publications Inc., 1996), 67.

2. Thomas à Kempis, *The Imitation of Christ,* 123.

3. R. J. Deferrari, ed., *The Fathers of the Church,* vol. 26 of *Saint Ambrose Letters* (New York: Fathers of the Church Inc., 1954), 401.

4. A. C. Outler, ed., *The Confessions of St. Augustine,* 206.

5. Quoted in I. Delio, *Franciscan Prayer,* 48.

6. Ibid., 94.

ENDNOTES

7. Quoted in T. G. Weinandy & D. A. Keating, eds., *The Theology of St. Cyril of Alexandria: A Critical Appreciation* (London: T. & T. Clark, 2003), 174.

8. R. C. Petry, ed., "The Mending of Life," in *Late Medieval Mysticism,* vol. 13, 213.

9. R. B. Blakney, trans., *Meister Eckhart,* 88.

10. Helen Waddell, trans., *The Desert Fathers,* 108.

11. C. Luibheid, trans., *John Cassian: Conferences* (New York: Paulist Press, 1985), 107.

12. O. Davies, trans., "Patrick's Declaration of the Great Gifts of God," in *Celtic Spirituality, The Classics of Western Spirituality* (New York: Paulist Press, 1999), 82.

13. R. C. Petry, ed., "The Sparkling Stone," in *Late Medieval Mysticism,* vol. 13, 302.

14. B. Ward, trans., *The Prayers and Meditations of Saint Anselm,* 241.

15. R. J. Foster & J. B. Smith, eds., "The Dialogue," in *Devotional Classics,* 290.

16. Thomas à Kempis, *The Imitation of Christ,* 67.

17. *Celebrating Common Prayer: A Version of the Daily Office SSF* (London: Continuum, 1992), 261.

18. Quoted in B. P. Holt, *Thirsty for God: A Brief History of Christian Spirituality* (Minneapolis: Augsburg, 1993), 42.

19. D. J. Sheerin, *The Eucharist, Message of the Church Fathers,* vol. 7 (Wilmington: Michael Glazier, 1986), 152.

ENDNOTES

Chapter 4

1. Quoted in I. Delio, *Franciscan Prayer,* 48.

2. H. Betteson, ed., "The Rule of S. Francis, 1233," in *Documents of the Christian Church,* 2nd ed. (London: Oxford University Press, 1967), 128.

3. Bonaventure, *The Life of St. Francis, Harper Collins Spiritual Classics* (New York: HarperOne, 2005) 110.

4. Ibid., 94.

5. Jacopone da Todi, *Lauds, The Classics of Western Spirituality* (London: SPCK, 1982), 117.

6. B. Ward, trans., *The Prayers and Meditations of Saint Anselm,* 237.

7. Richard of St. Victor, *The Twelve Patriarchs, The Mystical Ark, Book Three of the Trinity, The Classics of Western Spirituality* (New York: Paulist Press, 1979), 322.

8. E. Griffin, ed., *Bernard of Clairvaux: Selected Works* (New York: HarperSanFrancisco, 2005), 88–89.

9. R. C. Petry, ed., *Late Medieval Mysticism,* vol. 13, 235.

10. Quoted in B. P. Holt, *Thirsty for God,* 64.

11. B. Ward, trans., *The Prayers and Meditations of Saint Anselm,* 132.

12. B. McGinn, ed., "Sermons on the Song of Songs, 83," in *The Essential Writings of Christian Mysticism* (New York: The Modern Library, 2006), 259.

13. R. B. Blakney, trans., *Meister Eckhart,* 188.

14. Thomas à Kempis, *The Imitation of Christ,* 83.

15. C. Luibheid, trans., *John Cassian: Conferences,* 50–51.

16. B. McGinn, ed., "The Little Book of Enlightenment," in *The Essential Writings of Christian Mysticism,* 449–450.

17. R. B. Blakney, trans., *Meister Eckhart,* 188.

18. Bonaventure, *The Life of Francis,* 94.

19. B. Ward, trans., *The Prayers and Meditations of Saint Anselm,* 145–146.

20. A. C. Outler, ed., *The Confessions of St. Augustine,* 88.

21. Quoted in B. McGinn, *The Growth of Mysticism, The Presence of God: A History of Western Mysticism,* vol. 2 (London: SCM Press, 1995), 108.

22. Quoted in I. Delio, *Franciscan Prayer,* 28–29.

23. Quoted in P. Evdokimov, *Ages of the Spiritual Life,* 195.

24. Quoted in T. G. Weinandy & D. A. Keating, eds., *The Theology of St. Cyril of Alexandria,* 174.

25. William of St. Thierry, *The Nature and Dignity of Love, Cistercian Fathers Series,* no. 30 (Kalamazoo: Cistercian Publications, 1981), 100.

26. B. Ward, trans., *The Prayers and Meditations of Saint Anselm,* 103.

27. Quoted in B. P. Holt, *Thirsty for God,* 31.

28. T. Fry, ed., *The Rule of St. Benedict* (New York: Vintage Books, 1998), 12.

ENDNOTES

29. S. L. Greenslade, ed., "Unity of the Catholic Church," in *Early Latin Theology, The Library of Christian Classics* (Louisville: Westminster, 1956), 127.

Chapter 5

1. B. Ward, trans., *The Prayers and Meditations of Saint Anselm,* 212.

2. Quoted in L. S. Cunningham and K. J. Egan, *Christian Spirituality: Themes from the Tradition* (New York: Paulist Press, 1996), 171–172.

3. E. de Waal, *Seeking God: The Way of St. Benedict* (Collegeville: The Liturgical Press, 1984), 116.

4. Thomas à Kempis, *The Imitation of Christ,* 30.

5. William of St. Thierry, *The Nature and Dignity of Love,* 100.

6. Quoted in D. J. Sheerin, *The Eucharist,* 152.

7. Ibid., 324.

8. B. Ward, trans., *The Prayers and Meditations of Saint Anselm,* 101.

9. H. Waddell, trans., *The Desert Fathers,* 134.

10. Julian of Norwich, *Revelations of Divine Love,* 204.

11. W. Johnston, ed., *The Cloud of Unknowing,* 153.

12. C. C. Richardson, ed., "Clement's First Letter," in *Early Christian Fathers,* vol. 1 of *The Library of Christian Classics* (Philadelphia: The Westminster Press, 1953), 54.

ENDNOTES

13. "Revelations of Divine Love," in R. J. Foster & J. B. Smith, *Devotional Classics,* 71.

14. B. Ward, trans., *The Prayers and Meditations of Saint Anselm,* 95.

15. H. W. Holmes, ed., *The Apostolic Fathers in English,* 3rd ed. (Grand Rapids: Baker Academic, 2006), 296.

16. Helen Waddell, trans., *The Desert Fathers,* 81.

17. Thomas à Kempis, *The Imitation of Christ,* 15.

18. R. B. Blakney, trans., *Meister Eckhart,* 57.

19. B. Ward, trans., *The Prayers and Meditations of Saint Anselm,* 150.

20. R. B. Blakney, trans., *Meister Eckhart,* 90.

21. A. C. Outler, ed., *The Confessions of Saint Augustine,* 195.

22. C. Luibhead, trans., *John Cassian: Conferences,* 164.

23. E. Spearing, ed., "The Mirror of Simple Souls," in *Medieval Writings on Female Spirituality,* 141.

Chapter 6

1. Quoted in A. Curtayne, *Saint Catherine of Siena* (Rockford, IL: Tan, 1980), 48.

2. H. W. Holmes, ed., "The Letter of Polycarp to the Philippians," in *The Apostolic Fathers in English,* 140.

3. Quoted in E. Underhill, *The Spiritual Life* (London: Hodder & Stoughton, 1937), 99.

ENDNOTES

4. A. C. Outler, ed., *The Confessions of St. Augustine,* 139.

5. Thomas à Kempis, *The Imitation of Christ,* 108.

6. S. L. Greenslade, ed., "Letter 108: To Eustochium," in *Early Latin Theology,* 350.

7. C. Luibeid, trans., *John Cassian: Conferences,* 107.

8. R. J. Foster & J. B. Smith, eds., "Theologia Germanica," in *Devotional Classics,* 149.

9. Quoted in P. Evdokimov, *Ages of the Spiritual Life,* 208.

10. B. McGinn, ed., "Sermon 39," in *The Essential Writings of Christian Mysticism,* 106.

Chapter 7

1. S. L. Greenslade, ed., "Letters," in *Early Latin Theology,* 296.

2. C. Luibheid, trans., *John Cassian: Conferences,* 73.

3. A. Roberts & J. Donaldson, eds., "The Epistles of Cyprian," in vol. 5 of *The Ante-Nicene Fathers* (Edinburgh: T. & T. Clark, 1995), 287.

4. E. Griffen, ed., *Hildegard of Bingen: Selections from Her Writings,* 110.

5. H. Waddell, trans., *The Desert Fathers,* 81.

6. J. J. O'Meara, trans., *Origen, Ancient Christian Writers,* no. 19 (New York: Newman Press, 1954), 125.

7. Quoted in P. Evdokimov, *Ages of the Spiritual Life,* 190.

8. Thomas à Kempis, *The Imitation of Christ,* 103.

9. Quoted in M. H. Crosby, *Finding Francis, Following Christ* (Maryknoll: Orbis Books, 2007), 86.

10. Quoted in D. J. Sheerin, *The Eucharist,* 152.

11. B. Ward, trans., *The Prayers and Meditations of Saint Anselm,* 212.

Chapter 8

1. R. B. Blakney, trans., *Meister Eckhart,* 154.

2. W. Johnston, ed., *The Cloud of Unknowing,* 79.

3. B. McGinn, ed., "The Mind's Journey into God," in *The Essential Writings of Christian Mysticism,* 164–165.

4. E. Spearing, ed., "The Life of St. Mary of Oignies," in *Medieval Writings on Female Spirituality,* 102.

5. Thomas à Kempis, *The Imitation of Christ,* 26.

6. Quoted in B. P. Holt, *Thirsty for God,* 64.

7. Quoted in I. Delio, *Franciscan Prayer,* 130.

8. W. Johnston, ed., *The Cloud of Unknowing,* 60.

9. B. Ward, trans., *The Prayers and Meditations of Saint Anselm,* 219.

10. Quoted in K. Leech, *Soul Friend: A Study of Spirituality* (London: Sheldon Press, 1977), 38.

11. William of St. Thierry, *The Nature and Dignity of Love,* 97.

ENDNOTES

12. Quoted in L. S. Cunningham & K. G. Egan, *Christian Spirituality*, 91.

13. Quoted in J. Leclercq, *The Love of Learning and the Desire for God*, 284.

14. Quoted in I. Delio, *Franciscan Prayer*, 48.

Chapter 9

1. C. C. Richardson, ed., "The Teaching of the Twelve Apostles, Commonly Called the Didache," in *Early Christian Fathers*, vol. 1 of *The Library of Christian Classics* (Philadelphia: The Westminster Press, 1953), 173.

2. Quoted in P. Evdokimov, *Ages of the Spiritual Life*, 137.

3. A. C. Outler, ed., *The Confessions of St. Augustine*, 101.

4. H. Waddell, trans., *The Desert Fathers*, 160.

5. H. W. Holmes, ed., *The Apostolic Fathers in English*, 296.

6. Ibid., 180.

7. G. C. Berthold, trans., "The Four Hundred Chapters on Love," in *Maximus Confessor: Selected Writings, The Classics of Western Spirituality* (London: SPCK, 1985), 38.

8. E. de Waal, *Seeking God: The Way of St. Benedict*, 116.

9. C. C. Richardson, ed., "Clements First Letter," in *Early Church Fathers*, vol. 1, 54.

10. H. W. Holmes, ed., *The Apostolic Fathers in English*, 295.

ENDNOTES

11. S. L. Greenslade, ed., "Letter 41: The Synagogue at Callinicum," in *Early Latin Theology,* 247.

12. Quoted in C. Mathewes, *A Theology of Public Life* (Cambridge: Cambridge University Press, 2007), 92.

13. H. Bettenson, ed., "The Rule of St. Francis, 1223," in *Documents of the Christian Church,* 128.

14. A. C. Outler, ed., *The Confessions of St. Augustine,* 101.

15. R. B. Blakney, trans., *Meister Eckhart,* 157.

16. H. W. Holmes, ed., "Letter of Ignatius to the Ephesians," in *The Apostolic Fathers in English,* 100.

17. C. C. Richardson, ed., "The Teaching of the Twelve Apostles, Commonly Called the Didache," in *Early Church Fathers,* 173.

18. H. Waddell, trans., *The Desert Fathers,* 128.

19. R. C. Petry, ed., "The Mending of Life," in *Late Medieval Mysticism,* vol. 13, 231.

Chapter 10

1. Quoted in I. Delio, *Franciscan Prayer,* 150.

2. Quoted in B. Holt, *Thirsty for God: A Brief History of Christian Spirituality,* 42.

3. Quoted in G. L. Sittner, *Water from a Deep Well: Spirituality from Early Martyrs to Modern Missionaries* (Downers Grove: IVP, 2007), 133.

ENDNOTES

4. P. Schaff, ed., *Nicene and Post-Nicene Fathers,* vol. 9 of *Chrysostom: On the Priesthood, Ascetic Practices, Select Homilies and Letters, and Homilies on the Statues, A Select Library of the Christian Church* (Peabody: Hendrickson Publishers, 1994), 343.

5. Thomas à Kempis, *The Imitation of Christ,* 90.

6. R. B. Blakney, trans., *Meister Eckhart,* 157.

7. W. Johnston, ed., *The Cloud of Unknowing,* 156.

8. G. C. Berthold, trans., "The Four Hundred Chapters on Love," in *Maximus Confessor: Selected Writings,* 38.

9. Quoted in D. G. Groody, *Globalization, Spirituality and Justice: Navigating the Path to Peace* (Maryknoll: Orbis Books, 2007), 67.

10. Quoted in D. G. Groody, *Globalization, Spirituality and Justice,* 67.

11. Ibid., 71.

12. Ibid.

13. Ibid., 69.

14. C. Jones, G. Wainwright, E. Yarnold, eds., *The Study of Spirituality* (New York: Oxford University Press, 1986), 222.

15. Quoted in K. Leech, *Soul Friend: A Study of Spirituality,* 41.

16. Ibid., 55–56.

17. Quoted in B. Holt, *Thirsty for God,* 42.

18. E. Griffin, ed., *Hildegard of Bingen: Selections from Her Writings,* 47.

19. Quoted in I. Delio, *Franciscan Prayer,* 185.

ENDNOTES

Chapter 11

1. Thomas à Kempis, *The Imitation of Christ,* 15.

2. B. Ward, trans., *The Prayers and Meditations of Saint Anselm,* 95.

3. W. Johnston, ed., *The Cloud of Unknowing,* 156.

4. Quoted in M. Fox, ed., *Western Spirituality: Historical Roots, Ecumenical Routes,* 229.

5. B. Ward, trans., *The Prayers and Meditations of Saint Anselm,* 98.

6. S. L. Greenslade, ed., "Letters," in *Early Latin Theology,* 296.

7. A. C. Outler, ed., *The Confessions of St. Augustine,* 90.

8. B. Ward, trans., *The Prayers and Meditations of Saint Anselm,* 132.

9. A. C. Outler, ed., *The Confessions of St. Augustine,* 252.

10. E. Spearing, ed., "Poem 17," in *Medieval Writings on Female Spirituality,* 57.

11. E. Spearing, ed., "Letters," in *Medieval Writings on Female Spirituality,* 48.

12. E. Spearing, ed., "The Mirror of Simple Souls," in *Medieval Writings on Female Spirituality,* 141.

13. Quoted in P. Evdokimov, *Ages of the Spiritual Life,* 195.

14. R. J. Foster & J. B. Smith, eds., "Revelations of Divine Love," in *Devotional Classics,* 70.

ENDNOTES

15. T. Fry, ed., *The Rule of St. Benedict,* 12.

16. E. Griffen, ed., *Hildegard of Bingen: Selections from Her Writings,* 129.

17. O. Davies, trans., "Sermons of Columbanus," in *Celtic Spirituality,* 358.

18. E. Griffin, ed., "On Loving God," in *Bernard of Clairvaux: Selected Works,* 79–80.

19. Quoted in B. P. Holt, *Thirsty for God: A Brief History of Christian Spirituality,* 64.

20. H. Waddell, trans., *The Desert Fathers,* 134.

21. B. Ward, trans., *The Prayers and Meditations of Saint Anselm,* 103.

22. Quoted in T. G. Weinandy & D. A. Keating, eds., *The Theology of St. Cyril of Alexandria: A Critical Appreciation,* 174.

23. Quoted in A. Hyma, *The Brethren of the Common Life,* 60.

Chapter 12

1. Quoted in D. Allen, *Spiritual Theology* (Cambridge, MA: Cowley Publications, 1997), 154–155.

2. Thomas à Kempis, *The Imitation of Christ,* 26.

3. E. Griffen, ed., *Bernard of Clairvaux: Selected Works,* 5.

4. E. Griffen, ed., *Hildegard of Bingen: Selections from Her Writings,* 129.

ENDNOTES

5. P. Schaff and H. Wace, eds., "De Spiritu Sancto," in *Nicene and Post-Nicene Fathers of the Christian Church,* vol. 8 of *St. Basil: Letters and Select Works* (Grand Rapids: Eerdmans, 1989), 15.

6. "De Spiritu Sancto," 16.

7. B. Ward, trans., *The Prayers and Meditations of Saint Anselm,* 150.

8. S. L. Greenslade, ed., "Letter 41: The Synagogue at Callinicum," in *Early Latin Theology,* 247.

9. T. Fry, ed., *The Rule of St. Benedict,* 12.

10. B. Ward, trans., *The Prayers and Meditations of Saint Anselm,* 150.

11. R. J. Deferrari, ed., *The Fathers of the Church,* vol. 26 of *Saint Ambrose Letters,* 401.

12. *Celtic Daily Prayer from the Northumbria Community* (New York: HarperOne, 2002), 22.

www.ingramcontent.com/pod-product-compliance
Lightning Source LLC
Chambersburg PA
CBHW032039150426
43194CB00006B/341